The Forgotten
Players

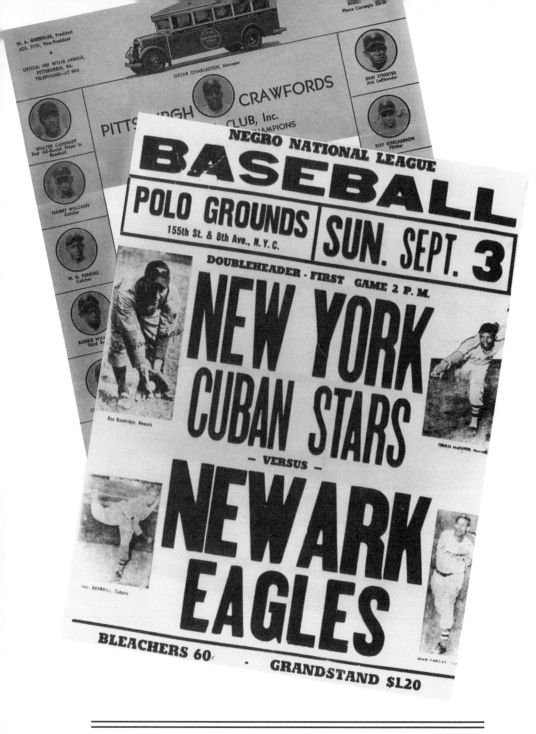

The Forgotten Players

The Story of Black Baseball in America

Robert Gardner
and
Dennis Shortelle

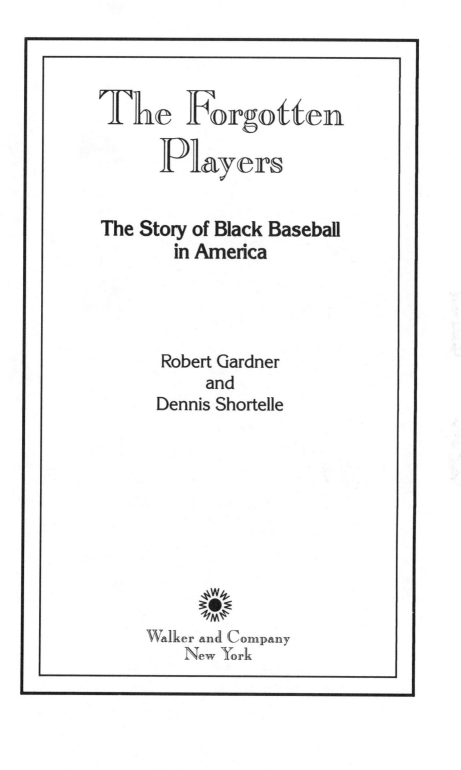

Walker and Company
New York

First published in the United States of America in 1993
by Walker Publishing Company, Inc.

Published simultaneously in Canada by Thomas Allen & Son
Canada, Limited, Markham, Ontario

Library of Congress Cataloging-in-Publication Data
Gardner, Robert, 1929–
The forgotten players: the story of black baseball in America / Robert
Gardner and Dennis Shortelle.
p.   cm.
Published simultaneously in Canada.
Summary: Traces the history of the Negro leagues that evolved due to
segregation in professional baseball and the experiences of black
players from the late nineteenth through the early twentieth century.
ISBN 0-8027-8248-5 (c). — ISBN 0-8027-8249-3 (r)
1. Baseball—United States—History. 2. Negro leagues—History.
3. Discrimination in sports—United States—History. [1. Negro
leagues. 2. Baseball—History. 3. Afro-Americans—Biography.
4. Discrimination in sports.] I. Shortelle, Dennis. II. Title.
GV863.A1G39   1993
796.357'0973—dc20   92-29618
CIP
AC

Text Design by Georg Brewer

Printed in the United States of America

2   4   6   8   10   9   7   5   3   1

CONTENTS

The Forgotten Players

INTRODUCTION

Organized baseball, long regarded as America's national pastime, has only recently accepted its responsibility for neglecting a group of outstanding but forgotten players. Though many were qualified, these players were denied the opportunity to play major league baseball and admission to the Baseball Hall of Fame because their skin was black.

In the early years of organized baseball, more than a century ago, a few black men played on predominantly white professional teams. Players long forgotten—Bud Fowler, Frank Grant, and Fleetwood Walker—were recognized as having major league talent. But by 1900 the game had become a microcosm of America's segregated society. Those who managed organized baseball had informally agreed to bar black men from the major leages.

The most common statement presented by major league owners to explain their refusal to hire black players was that southern whites would never play on or against integrated teams. This may have been true in the early part of the century through the racially tense 1920s. But by the 1930s and 1940s, when major league all-star teams regularly barnstormed about the country competing against the best teams in the Negro leagues, the logic in such an explanation seemed flawed.

The most outrageous argument offered by owners was that there were no qualified black players. The sentiment of the owners was not shared by many of the major leaguers who played against black players in the off season. They stated clearly that Josh Gibson, Smokey Joe Williams, Chino

Smith, Satchel Paige, Ray Dandridge, and a number of others were as good as, if not better than, the top players in the majors. Their evaluation is confirmed by records of 432 barnstorming games between blacks and white major league all-stars, which reveal that blacks won 266 games, whites 166.

Once the color barrier was broken in 1947, the play of such black stars as Jackie Robinson, Roy Campanella, Don Newcombe, Larry Doby, Monte Irvin, and others made it clear that outstanding black players were not hard to find and that they were often better than their white teammates. Indeed, an analysis of the statistics from 1947 to 1960 for all white, black, and Hispanic players showed that for an average 550 at bats, white players batted .262, with thirteen home runs and four stolen bases. Black players batted .280, with twenty homers and ten stolen bases. Hispanic players batted .267, with ten home runs and eleven steals. Of course, in this era only the very best black players were playing in the major leagues. Consequently, these statistics are not surprising.

The real reasons for segregation were simple. The owners of major league teams, like most of white America, had no interest in integrating the game. Besides, with segregated baseball, owners made extra money by renting their stadiums to black teams. By the 1930s and 1940s any memory of black players in organized baseball had been forgotten. The major leagues had been white since 1900. As far as the owners were concerned, segregation in the major leagues was an established tradition. Owners discouraged one another from signing black men. They knew that if a maverick owner signed a superb black player, that team would have an advantage in securing other outstanding black performers. (Their anxiety in this matter was well founded. After Jackie Robinson joined the Brooklyn Dodgers organization in 1945, the Dodgers signed John Wright, Roy Partlow, Roy Campanella, and Don Newcombe within a year.)

After being banned from organized baseball for twenty years, black sportsmen, under the leadership of Rube Foster, formed their own Negro National League in 1920. The Negro National League was an association of major league–caliber teams composed of the best black players in the country. Teams in the Negro National League, with regularly scheduled games, stood in sharp contrast to the black teams found in the Texas and Southern Negro Leagues and independent teams such as the Mohawk Giants of Albany, New York. These "minor" league teams were mainly barnstorming clubs that roamed the countryside in search of competition.

Aside from serving as a showcase for accomplished athletes, the Negro leagues were a testimony to the role baseball played in the black culture of America. It was an opportunity for men from humble, rural, mostly southern backgrounds to achieve fame in a game they loved to play. Satchel Paige and Josh Gibson were notable examples of players who escaped the anonymity of baseball's apartheid. Dave Malarcher, the son of ex-slaves, became the manager of the most successful black team of his time, was recognized as a superb third baseman, and later developed a successful real estate business. Such men were proof that although barred and vilified, blacks, like other Americans, could aspire to and achieve a better life.

Black leagues served a social function as well. League games became the place to be seen on Sunday afternoons; home teams regularly drew crowds of 15,000 or more. This was particularly true of the four-team double headers in New

Effa Manley, queen of the Negro leagues. *Courtesy of Dr. Lawrence Hogan.*

York during the late 1930s and early 1940s. Effa Manley, wife of the owner of the Newark Eagles, recalled opening day as particularly festive: "And did they dress for opening day. People came out who didn't know the ball from the bat. All the girls got new outfits."[1]

According to Manley, in her book *Negro Baseball Before Integration*,[2] the leagues also had an important economic impact. Players were paid much more money than blacks in most other jobs, parks were rented, taxes were paid, and monies were spent for transportation, equipment, and incidentals. *The 1945 Negro Baseball Yearbook* estimated that Negro league baseball was a two-million-dollar-a-year operation and that salaries were higher than those paid major league players. Their figures may have been exaggerated, but in 1942 Satchel Paige was paid $37,000, more than four times that of the average major league player. Monte Irvin took a pay cut (from $6,500 to $5,000) when he left the Negro National League's Newark Eagles to sign on with the major league New York Giants in 1948.

Today, many of those who played in the various professional Negro leagues are dead. The fields where they toiled are now playgrounds, housing projects, or parking lots. Little is left to make the present generations aware of the leagues and the players that constituted black baseball during the first half of the twentieth century. With each passing day the throng of once-loyal fans steadily diminishes. Authors Janet Bruce, John Holway, Robert Peterson, and Donn Rogosin have kept the memories of black players alive; they have provided a new generation with a knowledge of black baseball. We have drawn from their work to provide young readers with a view of segregated baseball, a phenomenon that, happily, has disappeared from the American scene.

This book is not about how many games were won by pitchers like Satchel Paige, or how many home runs were slammed by Josh Gibson. Rather, it's about baseball players who, because of the color of their skin, were banned from major league baseball. It's about their lives in a game they played because they loved it, a game they played to keep the path open for those who eventually broke the barrier that had divided professional baseball into black and white leagues for half a century.

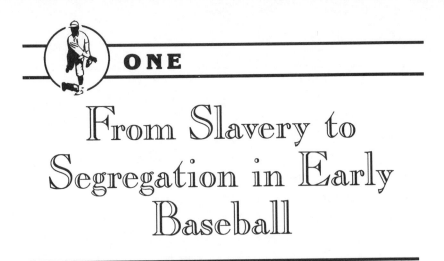

ONE

From Slavery to Segregation in Early Baseball

I f you go to a major league baseball game today, you'll find the lineup consists of black and white men in whatever order the manager thinks will produce the most runs. Before 1947 there was not a single black man on any major league team. And it was 1959 before every major league team had at least one black player on its roster.

Black Players in the Early Years of Baseball

Before the Civil War (1861–1865), slavery was legal in the United States. Black men and women were transported to the United States from Africa and sold like cattle. Most slaves worked in southern fields, where they planted and harvested cotton and other crops for their owners. Some were domestic servants, but all were regarded as property.

In September 1862, President Abraham Lincoln issued the Emancipation Proclamation. On January 1, 1863, all slaves in the states that had seceded from the union were to become free.

During the last few months of the war, and in the years immediately thereafter, the Thirteenth, Fourteenth, and Fifteenth amendments abolished slavery throughout the nation and gave blacks their citizenship. However, what was given in theory was never fully given in practice by the nation's white citizens, and certainly not by baseball players and owners of professional teams. For example, individual groups such as the National Association of Base Ball Players (NABBP), a loose confederation of teams primarily concerned with the rules of the game, barred from membership any club with one or more colored persons. In 1871, the National Association of Professional Base Ball Players (NAPBBP) banned blacks too. Despite such regulations within these associations, records reveal that a few black men played the game with whites in a number of early professional and semiprofessional leagues.

John W. ("Bud") Fowler, born in 1854 in Cooperstown, New York, was the first of about thirty blacks who played in predominantly white professional leagues before 1900. Fowler played for the New Castle, Pennsylvania, team as early as 1872. By 1884 there were eleven leagues under national agreement; that is, the teams in these leagues promised not to raid other teams under the same accord. The four strongest leagues under this agreement were the National Association, the American Association, the Eastern League, and the North Western League. By this time, Fowler was playing for Stillwater, Minnesota, in the North Western League. Press reports indicated that he was one of the best players in the nation, but many clubs would not hire him because of his color.

In 1886, another black player, Frank Grant, broke into professional baseball with Meriden, Connecticut, in the Eastern League; his batting average was .325 in thirty-three games. When the club folded, as teams often did in those days, he moved on to play forty-five games for Buffalo. There he batted .340 and was described by *Sporting Life* magazine as the best all-around player ever to have performed in Buffalo.

Two years later, Grant led Buffalo in batting, but his fellow players refused to sit with him for a team photograph. Such prejudice could be seen on the field as well. Grant and other blacks were subject to far more spikings and bean balls than white players. Sports writers credited Grant with inventing shin guards, which he wore while playing second base. He wore them as a defense against the sharpened spikes of base stealers who deliberately attempted to cut him. Often, the first man to attempt a steal would try to split Grant's wooden shin guards in an effort to leave him at the mercy of base stealers who followed. Toward the end of his career, Grant wisely took an outfield position far from the high-flying spikes of opposing players.

In 1884, Moses ("Fleetwood") Walker became the first black man to play in what were then considered the major leagues. He caught and batted .251 for Toledo of the American Association. Although he lacked the athletic skills of Grant and Fowler, he was a graduate of Oberlin College and certainly better educated than most of the players of the day, black or white. Fans, reflecting society's attitude toward blacks, hissed Walker when Toledo played in Louisville. Players were no better. The Richmond team threatened a riot if Walker attempted to play there. The riot never occurred because Walker broke a rib before the series began. In those days catchers did not wear chest protectors; a foul ball into the ribs was one of the hazards of the position.

Later that year, Walker was released by Toledo, but he continued to play professional baseball with several other teams until 1889. After leaving baseball, he held a number of jobs and eventually became editor of *The Equator,* a Stubenville, Ohio, newspaper. He also wrote a small book entitled *Our Home Colony—A Treatise on the Past, Present, and Future of the Negro Race in America.* Scarred by the injustice he had encountered both in and out of baseball, Walker rejected the idea that education, religion, hard work, intermarriage, or anything else could put an end to racial prejudice. Instead, he recommended, as had Abraham Lincoln, that blacks emigrate back to Africa and establish new colonies there. He saw no hope for blacks in America.

Jim Crow Enters Baseball

Jim Crow was a minstrel character popular before the Civil War who represented the supposedly happy slave. As race relations changed after the war, "Jim Crow" became a euphemism for segregation. Legal segregation arose when states passed laws preventing blacks and whites from using the same hotels, theaters, restaurants, schools, waiting rooms, bathrooms, and even drinking fountains. These "Jim Crow" laws were upheld by the United States Supreme Court in the 1896 *Plessy* v. *Ferguson* decision. The court ruled that "separate but equal" facilities for blacks did not violate their constitutional rights. In reality, the facilities available to blacks were separate and inferior.

During this same period, baseball became increasingly segregated too. An event in 1887 triggered the end of integrated professional baseball. George Stovey, a black pitcher who was the ace of the Newark Little Giants, was scheduled to pitch against the Chicago White Stockings. Just before the game, the Newark manager scratched Stovey from the lineup. Cap Anson, the Babe Ruth of his time, had threatened that he and his White Stockings teammates would not play if Stovey pitched. Rather than lose the proceeds from a game that attracted a large crowd, the manager agreed to use a white pitcher.

Three years later, at a hotel in Wilmington, Delaware, Frank Grant was told he could not register with his Harrisburg teammates. At another hotel in the same city, Grant was given a room but told he could not eat in the dining room. He would have to dine in the kitchen with the black employees or eat elsewhere.

The Anson-Stovey affair and the Frank Grant incident reflected white society's attitude toward blacks in post–Civil War America. A statement in 1895 by Booker T. Washington, the great black educator, indicated that many blacks were willing to accept less than full citizenship: "In all things that are purely social we can be as separate as the five fingers, yet one as the hand in all things essential to mutual progress."

Washington accepted Jim Crowism as the best that blacks could hope for at that time. He advocated an education for blacks that stressed practical learning. By developing the skills needed for farming and industry, argued Washington, blacks could take advantage of the jobs open to them. He believed that thrift, patience, perseverance, good morals, and good manners would lead to worthwhile employment in a society controlled by whites. With good jobs, black men could acquire property and build an economic base from which to grow.

Although Washington's views were strongly opposed by thinkers like W. E. B. Du Bois, who advocated true equality for blacks, he was hailed by whites in both the North and South as a man who saw that only by accepting the system could blacks hope to succeed. What they did not realize was that Washington viewed his approach as a step along a path leading ultimately to equality and integration. Although he played down voting rights, Washington saw building an energetic, educated black population with a strong economic foundation as the way to acquire political strength.

Booker T. Washington's point of view became as evident in professional baseball as in society. Although no "Jim Crow" laws governed baseball, the game became every bit as segregated as the rest of society.

The First Professional Black Team

While both Cooperstown, New York, and Hoboken, New Jersey, claim to be the birthplace of baseball, the actual origin, like much of the early history of the game, is surrounded by myth and speculation. However, baseball historians do generally agree that professional black baseball teams were first seen in the 1880s. The earliest was the Athletics, a team organized by Frank P. Thompson, headwaiter and team manager at the Argyle Hotel in Babylon on New York's Long Island. It consisted of waiters who doubled as ball players. These waiters soon learned that Thompson was more interested in their skills on the field than in the dining room.

After a long summer home stand, which involved entertaining the guests at the resort by playing visiting white teams, Thompson's nine went on the road in October to meet opponents from the white major leagues. The team was purchased by Walter Cook, who brought them to Trenton, New Jersey, changing the name to the Cuban Giants—"Cuban" to conceal their racial backgrounds, and "Giants" because the New York Giants were a very popular major league team in the area. On the field, Cook encouraged his players to speak a gibberish that he hoped fans would assume was Spanish.

Within a year, Cook hired many of the best amateur

The Cuban Giants, probably the first black professional baseball team, originally consisted of waiters from the Argyle Hotel in Babylon, New York, in 1885. *Courtesy of Larry Lester/Negro Leagues Baseball Museum, Inc.*

and semipro black players from teams across the country. He turned down an offer to join the white Eastern League because it would interfere with the profitable Sunday games he scheduled with college, minor league, and major league teams. The quality of the team is evident from the fact that in 1887, the Cuban Giants were leading the World Champion Detroit Tigers 4–2 going into the eighth inning. Unfortunately, they booted the game with several costly errors and lost 6–4.

By 1890, there were a number of black teams throughout the East and South. Although few of them could match the Cuban Giants in talent, their increasing number reflected the fact that baseball was fast becoming segregated.

White Supremacy: In the Voting Booth and on the Diamond

Following passage of the Fifteenth Amendment in 1870, the Republican Party sought to build strength in the South by enrolling black voters. However, the Ku Klux Klan, the Knights of the White Camelia, and other racist organizations devised ways to establish white supremacy. Their methods were less subtle and more violent than those used in professional baseball. By intimidation, force, arson, bribery, and murder, black men in many southern towns were kept from voting. Blacks who did vote were chased, whipped, maimed, or hanged. Other, less violent, communities placed polling booths far from black neighborhoods and blocked roads or closed ferries on election days. Some simply stuffed the ballot boxes.

In 1876, the white supremacy movement gained support from the Supreme Court. In *The United States* v. *Cruikshank*, the Court ruled that the Fifteenth Amendment did not guarantee the right to vote but only a right not to be discriminated against by states because of race, color, or previous condition of servitude. This ruling allowed southern states to pass laws that required voters to pay a poll tax; pass a literacy test that required an ability to read, write, and interpret the state constitution; or own (in some states) at least $300 worth of property. Since southern blacks were generally poor, illiterate, and without property, most of them were excluded from voting.

In 1896, there were 130,000 registered black voters in Louisiana. In 1900, after new voting laws were established, only 5,000 blacks remained eligible to vote. In Alabama, new voting laws reduced the number of registered black voters from 180,000 to 3,000.

Organized baseball had never seen large numbers of blacks dash onto the playing fields, but the exclusion of black players from professional baseball was to be more complete than the elimination of black voters from the polls. As the racist grumblings of Cap Anson and other white players grew louder, the directors of the International League ruled that after 1887 new contracts would be issued only to

The Page Fence Giants of Adrian, Michigan, a successful black team that combined showmanship with skill, shown astride their sponsor's product. *Courtesy of Larry Lester/Negro Leagues Baseball Museum, Inc.*

white players. The five black players already in the league were exempted from the ruling, but by 1901, when the American League was organized (the National League had existed since 1876), not a single black player wore the uniform of a major or a minor league team. Neither major league had a rule barring blacks from participating, but white players and owners had an understanding; the game was to be played by whites. Banished from white baseball, blacks who loved the game did the only thing they could: they formed their own separate but "equal" black teams and eventually their own leagues.

Rube Foster and the Negro National League

A ndrew "Rube" Foster's belated admission to the Baseball Hall of Fame in 1981 was an honor well deserved. It was Foster, more than anyone else, who promoted black baseball. In addition to being a star pitcher and manager, he was a legendary tutor of successful white pitchers and a friend to owners of major league teams. His work in promoting black baseball, developing its unique style of play, and perfecting the skills of its players were essential to the success and stature of the black leagues that evolved through his efforts. When the racial barriers finally fell after World War II, the players in the leagues Foster had worked so hard to develop had the ability and the confidence to compete successfully with white professionals.

Foster the Player

By the time he was eighteen, the young Texan had mastered a blazing fastball and a nasty screwball that he threw with a smooth, underhand delivery. He served his apprenticeship with a black team, the Texas Yellow Jackets, where he soon became the ace of this barnstorming club. His talents were recognized beyond Texas when he pitched

Rube Foster, father of the Negro leagues. *Courtesy of Larry Lester/Negro Leagues Baseball Museum, Inc.*

spring training batting practice for major league teams such as Connie Mack's Philadelphia Athletics.

In 1902, Frank Leland, owner of the Leland Giants, a black team from Chicago, signed Foster to a contract, giving him an opportunity to compete against some of the best black and white semipro teams in the country. In a letter to Leland, Foster wrote, "If you play the best clubs in the land as you say, it will be a case of great meeting great. I fear nobody."[1]

Despite his bravado, his pitching with the Leland Giants was uninspiring. In despair, a frustrated Foster looked eastward. He signed on with the Cuban Giants of Philadelphia for forty dollars a month and fifteen cents a day for meals. He took a 13–0 shellacking in his first outing, but his manager, E. B. Lamar, Jr., later recalled that his stint with the Cuban Giants in 1902 was a turning point in Foster's career.

Foster thought he knew more than anyone else and would take that giant windup with men on base. They ran wild and taught Rube a lesson. From then on he made a study of the game and every chance he got he would go out to the big league parks and watch big league clubs in action.[2]

Having learned his lesson, Foster evolved from thrower to pitcher that year and earned the nickname "Rube" by beating the pennant-winning Philadelphia A's and their ace pitcher, Rube Waddell, by a score of 5–2 in New York City.

By 1905, Rube Foster had secured a place in the annals of black baseball. In the unofficial "colored world championships" of 1904, he won four of five games for the Cuban Giants against their cross-town rivals, the Philadelphia Giants. The next year, he joined the team he had defeated and won fifty games for them. In the championship series that fall he won two of the three games he pitched and was the club's leading hitter. By 1906, many considered him to be the best pitcher in all of baseball—black or white. Honus Wagner, a future Hall of Famer, reputedly remarked that Foster was "the smoothest pitcher I've ever seen."[3]

According to legend, it was at about this time that Foster began a lifelong friendship with John McGraw, the feisty manager of the New York Giants, a well-established white major league team. Unable to sign Foster because of his color, McGraw hired him as an unofficial pitching coach. It was Foster who taught Hall of Famer Christy Matthewson to throw a "fadeaway"—a screwball.

In 1906 Foster was back in Chicago with the Leland Giants. Frank Leland was planning an entertainment complex on his property at Ninth and Wentworth. There would be a roller skating rink and bowling alleys, but the centerpiece would be the Leland Giants.[4] With his prize pitcher, Leland's club reigned supreme in the predominantly white Chicago city league. They won forty-eight games in a row and compiled an astounding season record of 110–10. Rube's contribution was recognized by the *Chicago Inter Ocean:*

> *Rube Foster is a pitcher with the tricks of Radbourne, with the speed of Rusie and with the coolness and deliberation of a Cy Young. What does that make him? Why the greatest baseball pitcher in the country— that's what the greatest baseball players of white per- suasion who have gone against him say. He would be a priceless boon to the struggling White Sox or the Highlanders.[5]*

Despite their success on the field, the players were poorly paid. At a Fourth of July game the entire team received only $150 for a doubleheader. Acting as team spokesman, Foster entered a new phase of his career. He persuaded Leland to allow him to do the booking in return for 40 percent of the ownership. "After some argument, Foster said, 'We got it and made $500 that day instead of the piffling $150.' From then on every team Foster played on got a fifty-fifty split of the gate until the formation of the Negro National League."[6]

Although he continued to pitch until 1915, Foster formed a partnership with John Schorling, a white Chicago tavern owner, in 1911. Together they created a new black team—the Chicago American Giants. As a team owner, Foster began a career that changed the nature of black baseball.

Foster and Schorling

Schorling was the son-in-law of Charles Comisky, owner of the Chicago White Sox. When Comisky moved his team to a new ballpark (which has now, eighty years later, been replaced by another new stadium), Schorling offered to lease the vacant facility, which had a seating capacity of 9,000. Despite Comisky's gloomy prediction for the black team, the American Giants held their own against the city's representation in the white major leagues, the White Sox and the Cubs, in the battle for fans. On one Sunday in 1911, when all three teams were at home, the Cubs drew 6,000, the White Sox played before 9,000 fans, and a standing-room-only crowd of 11,000 watched the American Giants.[7]

For 50¢ and free ice water, baseball fans could watch the best black team in the Midwest—a team that won 123 games against only 6 defeats in its first season. Foster would later call this team his best edition of the American Giants, a club that dominated midwestern black baseball throughout the period preceding America's entry into World War I.

Rube Foster's Negro National League

As America entered the post–World War I era, Foster's contributions to baseball became widely recognized. He had been an outstanding pitcher and field manager who had won acclaim from both the black and white worlds of segregated baseball. His executive skills were evident as he built outstanding teams while establishing a firm financial base for black baseball. Nevertheless, his greatest challenge and his finest achievement as the "Father of Negro Baseball" lay ahead.

After the war, teams scrambled for limited dollars, and raiding of talent from established teams became common. The American Giants, the most successful team in black baseball, was a prime target for raiding owners seeking to establish their own identity in the wide-open Negro circuit. Rube was well aware of such behavior because he himself had often followed the dollar, moving from team to team in search of better pay and competition. Nat Strong, a New York booking agent and owner of the Brooklyn Royal Giants, and Ed Bolden of the Hilldale, Pennsylvania, Daisies, were especially active in signing disaffected players. Their teams were comparable to Foster's in skills, in depth of talent, and in attracting fans. Foster described the situation in the *Chicago Defender,* one of the leading black newspapers of the day:

> *If you have taken your club [and] win many games the owners try to take men away from you, bring dissatis-*

faction between you and your men, so much so you
avoid going there. Ballplayers have had no respect for
their word, contracts, or moral obligations, yet they are
not nearly as much to blame as the different owners of
the clubs.[8]

A team playing "out of region" was an invitation for
owners to steal players from competing clubs. Consequently, the owners of the best teams were reluctant to travel
and play other outstanding opponents for fear of losing key
players. One author estimated that Satchel Paige, during his
great pitching career, wore the uniform of more than 250
teams, many for a single game. In fact, within the Negro
leagues Paige was as well known for jumping contracts as
for striking out opponents.

In 1920, Foster opened a campaign to create a national
Negro league similar to the white major leagues. Foster
sensed that the only way to make real money was to develop
intercity rivalries and a world series within the framework of
a stable nationwide organization of owners who would agree
not to raid opposing teams. He argued that such an association of teams would lead to the construction of new ballparks, player development, a stable schedule, better
competition, improved social status for the players, and
employment for blacks in baseball-related jobs such as
scouting, umpiring, and other auxiliary businesses. Most
important, it would provide investment opportunities for the
rising black middle class.[9]

On February 13, 1920, despite little support from eastern owners such as Nat Strong, the owners of the top
western teams met in Kansas City and established the Negro
National League. Each team put up $500 to police league
bylaws and establish an emergency fund. The league in-

cluded eight teams: the Cincinnati Cuban Stars and Chicago Giants (both strictly road teams because they had no home fields), Dayton Marcos, Detroit Stars, Indianapolis ABCs, Kansas City Monarchs, St. Louis Giants, and, of course, Foster's own Chicago American Giants.

Foster, who was elected league president, accepted the responsibility of directing the league, establishing a schedule, and arbitrating disputes while continuing to manage all phases of the game for his own team. Foster *was* the Negro National League.

The league opened on May 2, 1920, and throughout that first season games played in Chicago, Kansas City, and Indianapolis regularly drew crowds in excess of 8,000. However, the league's future was clouded by two problems that plagued black baseball throughout its history.

Problems

Many of the teams lacked stable financial support and knowledgeable management. After the first season, the Dayton team collapsed for lack of funds. The franchise was moved to Columbus, Ohio, where the team was known as the Buckeyes. According to Bill Foster, Rube's younger half-brother, much of the capital for both the Dayton and Columbus teams came from Foster's own pocket.[10]

The second problem was scheduling. Not one team owned its own park, and only the American Giants, the Detroit Stars, and an expansion team, the St. Louis Stars, were relatively independent because they leased their fields. Two teams had no home field. The remaining clubs rented minor league facilities and could play at home only when the team that owned the field was on the road.

Another scheduling difficulty involved each club's particular history. Many black teams had long-standing rivalries with local white semipro teams. These interracial games often drew larger crowds than league contests. Consequently, teams were reluctant to trade a game that was certain to bring in big money for a contest in a long-term scheme that might fail. As a result, many clubs in the Negro National League played fewer games with league teams than they did with opponents outside the circuit. For example, in 1921 the pennant-winning American Giants played sixty-two league games. The second-place Kansas City Monarchs played eighty-one games within the league, and the last-place Chicago Giants were involved in only forty-two official tilts.

Despite difficulties, Foster used the public press to defend and publicize the league. Comparisons with white major league teams were unrealistic, he argued, given the wealth and experience of these established organizations.[11] (While Foster's American Giants were comparable in talent and organization to major league teams, most black teams lacked sound financial resources.) He reminded readers that the league had survived and that it provided a variety of jobs for the communities involved. According to Foster, clubs spent $430,000 on salaries, $165,000 on parks, and $130,000 on transportation.[12] It seemed clear to him that economic self-interest alone should lead communities to support the newly established black league.

In 1921, after two seasons, Foster was more critical of the league. In a series of articles in the *Chicago Defender*, he criticized owners who had little business sense and a minimal knowledge of baseball. Too often, he maintained, these men listened to the press and to fans in developing strategy and obtaining players. Weak managers, he argued, instead of educating owners, often curried their favor by carrying out improper or foolish orders. Managers were often guilty too of giving preferential treatment to stars. Foster went on to criticize players whose behavior was often unprofessional, especially when they borrowed money from their employers or flaunted their newfound wealth.[13]

An Eastern Black League

Although the Negro National League under Foster's leadership had its problems, its many successes led owners of eastern black teams to form their own league in December of 1922. The Mutual Association of Eastern Colored Baseball Clubs, which they founded, was a six-team circuit composed of Nat Strong's Brooklyn Royal Giants, Ed Bolden's Hilldale club, the Lincoln Giants of New York, Atlantic City's Original Bacharach Giants, the Baltimore Black Sox, and Allessandro Pompez's Cuban All Stars.

The Eastern League was governed by six commissioners, one from each club, with Ed Bolton as chairman. The system never worked. Bolton, who was accused of favoritism, lacked the power to enforce decisions. Further, any real power resided unofficially with Nat Strong, the New York booking agent. While Strong owned the Royal Giants, his stranglehold on New York semipro baseball enabled him to control the Cuban Stars and the Bacharach Giants. As the *New York Age* observed, "It is often alleged that money is and always has been the one object of Mr. Strong in colored baseball."[14]

The creation of an eastern black league only increased the raiding of established midwestern teams. In 1924 the Indianapolis ABCs were decimated when ten players joined eastern teams. Even the American Giants lost their ace, Dave Brown, to New York's Lincoln Giants. Realizing that continued raiding could kill both leagues, Foster moved quickly. In a six-hour meeting in September 1924, a truce was reached. A formal agreement limiting the recruiting area for each league was signed three months later. Players under contract were forbidden to jump to another team without first receiving a formal release. It was also agreed that disputes would be settled by a three-man commission, one from each league and a third (independent) selected by the two league representatives.

The scheduling problems that confronted Foster were even more pronounced in the Eastern League. In addition, Strong's underhanded behavior, the lack of firm leadership, and conflicts between owners led to the collapse of the league in 1928.

In addition to interleague problems, Foster had to contend with discontent within his own team. At the end of the 1923 season, a number of American Giants players met secretly and drafted a letter to the *Chicago Defender*. The letter stated that they had lost the pennant because they had not put forth their best effort. The reason for their lackluster play, they claimed, was their owners' refusal to pay them what they were worth. Foster was furious. He opened his books to the newspaper. *Defender* reporters discovered that these players had been paid $1,100 more than their contracts called for. They found, too, that Foster had developed an incentive system for some of the better-known players and that he had split the gate receipts for spring training games with the players, something that not even major league clubs did. With the evidence in hand, the *Defender* blasted the dissident players for misrepresenting the facts. Clearly, Foster's competitive spirit was not limited to the field of play.

Rube Foster in Review

Foster's overall performance as manager, owner, and league director has been highly praised by veteran players and associates who worked with him and by scholars who have studied his life in detail.

Dave Malarcher, captain of the American Giants and Rube's able successor as team manager, knew Rube as well as anyone. He revealed that Foster had been offered lucrative contracts with a number of white semipro teams while he was an active pitcher. Rube turned down these offers because he felt an obligation to play in and help develop black baseball. He believed that baseball would someday be integrated. But without black players who could compete with whites, there would be no force to motivate such integration, and an opportunity for blacks to achieve equality would be lost.

Undoubtedly, Foster was ambitious for the league and for black baseball in general. According to legend, he met with John McGraw and National League president Ban Johnson in 1925 to try to schedule games between major league clubs and his American Giants when the white professionals had layovers or off days in Chicago. He also toyed with the idea of signing a white player to play for the American Giants. Unfortunately, Foster was not able to implement either idea.

As a manager, he was perhaps without equal. Recalling Rube's managerial skills, Malarcher, Foster's managerial successor, reminisced: "It isn't generally known but Rube was so superior in his knowledge of baseball that from 1920–22 we were so far out in front of the league by July they had to break the season up into two halves so there would be more interest in the league the second half."[15]

The team's success can be attributed to Foster's philosophy, personality, and dictatorial control. Discipline, attention to details, and intensity were the marks of a Foster-managed team. Any player lacking these qualities would find himself on one of the league's weaker teams the following season. Arthur Hardy, who pitched for Foster, recalled Rube's relationship with the players: "I wouldn't call him reserved, but he wasn't free and easy. You see Rube was a natural psychologist. Now he didn't know what psychology was and he probably couldn't fraternize and still maintain discipline; Rube was a strict disciplinarian. He wasn't harsh but he was strict. His dictums were not unreasonable, but if you broke one he'd clamp down on you."[16]

Retribution for miscues was immediate. Rube's son, Earl Foster, remembered one incident in which outfielder Jelly Gardner "was up to bunt, and he tripled. He came back and sat on the bench. The old man took that pipe he smoked—he always had it—and he popped him right across his head. And he fined him and told him, 'As long as I'm paying you, you'll do as I tell you to do.' "[17]

Ted Radcliffe, a batboy for the American Giants who later became a player, tells a similar story of Foster's directions to a pitcher. It seems that Rube ordered the pitcher to walk opposing slugger Oscar Charleston: "The guy didn't walk him and Charleston hit a home run. When he came into the clubhouse, Rube [swore at him and] said, 'That'll cost you $150, . . . when I tell you to walk a man, walk him.' "[18]

At the time that Babe Ruth's home run style of baseball was beginning to dominate the major leagues, Foster was developing a style of play that was to become the trademark of the Negro circuit. His was a technically sound, thoughtful, fast-moving, "tricky" style of play that relied on constant offensive pressure, speed, and the seldom-used bunt. It was a style that enabled Willie Wells to steal home with the winning run on successive days against a major league all-star team in the autumn of 1929. Although Foster's American Giants' hitting could not match that of the Kansas City Monarchs, who had five players with batting averages over .360, the Giants won three pennants as a result of Foster's style of play, a philosophy described here by Malarcher: "One thing he used to say: 'The element of surprise in baseball is like everything else. We do what the other fellow does not expect us to do.' This was his philosophy. This was why we did all those things. . . . He taught this; that in order for a man to put you out in going from base to base, the other team must make a perfect play. If you can run fast, he's got to make a play and if you surprise him he can't make a perfect play, he can't make it."[19]

Giving up a walk to a Foster team was equivalent to giving away a run because the bunt, steals, or squeeze plays that followed usually brought the runner across the plate. Foster controlled his men like a chessmaster. Each player had a role that best suited his particular talents. Taken individually, these players were not stars, but as a team they were the equal of any in the game. What he looked for were smart, disciplined players with speed afoot. According to Malarcher, seven men in the lineup could run the hundred-yard dash in ten seconds or less. Such men could effectively play Foster's bunt-and-run style of ball. In spring training he would draw a circle in front of home plate and make his players bunt into it. On July 4, 1921, the Indianapolis ABCs led the American Giants 18–0. Foster gave the bunt sign to eleven consecutive batters. The bunts, together with grand slams by slugger Christobel Torrienti and catcher Jim

Brown, enabled the Giants to catch up. The game, called by darkness, ended in an 18-all tie.

Foster's genius extended beyond the bunt-and-run to details that most managers had never considered. Frank Forbes, a former player, umpire, and promoter, and a member of the Baseball Hall of Fame selection committee, remembered: "We'd go out there to play . . . and you know what he does? We don't wise up until the end of the ball game, but he had drowned the . . . infield the night before. Those suckers lay down a bunt, it rolls nine feet and stops. The man's on. . . . By the time you got the ball he was on."[20]

James ("Cool Papa") Bell, who could round the bases in slightly more than thirteen seconds and is believed to be the fastest man ever to play the game, claimed that Foster used to build ridges along the foul lines to make sure that bunted balls stayed fair.

Foster would do anything he could to get that little extra edge. Bill Holland, an opposing pitcher, told of the master at his pregame best working on Oliver Marcelle, one of the Negro league's best third basemen. Rube strolled over to Marcelle and said: " 'They tell me you're a great third baseman.' Marcelle replied, 'Well, I do the best I can.' 'Well, we'll find out today. I got some racehorses out there; we'll lay down some bunts, see if you can field them.' The first one Marcelle missed, Foster said, 'I told you so.' "[21]

Outfielder Jelly Gardner tells a similar story: "He'd holler and tell the pitcher that the next fellow was going to bunt and they didn't believe him. But that's what would happen. Or he'd tell the third baseman 'Get ready to pick this one up.' Well the third baseman wouldn't believe it and sure enough there comes the bunt."[22]

Even off the field the search for the psychological edge made Foster's arrival a media event. George Sweatt, a Giants player who lived in an apartment above Foster, remembered Foster's method of ensuring sell-out crowds when the Giants played the Monarchs in Kansas City: "He liked to tell stories about what he was going to do to the Monarchs. He'd just brag and get crowds. They'd have to have the police come so traffic could move."[23]

Foster's Demise

In 1925 the Chicago American Giants finished fourth in the first half of the season and could do no better than third in the second half. Early in the 1926 season there was no improvement. Something was wrong with Foster. He had frequent memory lapses and difficulty recognizing people and places. George Sweatt remembered the night Rube cracked completely: "The night he went crazy—1926—we were sitting upstairs and his wife hollered, 'Oh no don't do that!' So I ran down and knocked on the door and said, 'Mrs. Foster, is there anything wrong?' She said, 'There's something wrong with Rube, he just going crazy down there. I'm going to have to call the law.' "[24]

Rube was placed in a state institution at Kankakee, Illinois. He lived four more years exiled far from the game he loved, raving about one more world series where he was needed to pitch. On December 9, 1930, Rube Foster died, at the age of fifty-one.

Judge W. C. Hueston, Foster's successor as league president, lacked the leadership to handle the problems that Foster had contained so effectively. Raiding by owners, players jumping contract, scheduling difficulties, and financial problems, compounded by the impact of the Great Depression, became increasingly common. In 1932, for the first time since 1920, there was no Negro National League schedule. Fortunately, new leadership emerged the following year, the league was resurrected, and fifteen years later Rube Foster's dream of integrated professional teams became a reality.

In testimony to his reputation and all he had done for the black people of America, his body lay in state for three days. Three thousand people stood outside a crowded funeral home to pay their last respects. The *Chicago Defender* summed it up well when they wrote that he "had died a martyr to the game, the most commanding figure baseball had ever known."[25] Years later, sportswriter Rick Roberts reflected:

> *He tried to get black baseball respectability. Otherwise the reservoir of black talent, which is the backbone of the major leagues today, might not have been there. Just might not have been there. Thirty-six of the boys in the Negro league went up to the majors, through the first fourteen years they dominated the Most Valuable Player votes in the National League in eleven of them, plus eight Rookie-of-the-Year awards in the first eleven years.*
>
> *That's Rube's greatest contribution, the organization, the perpetuation of black baseball.[26]*

THREE

Gus Greenlee and a New Negro League

The economic depression of the 1930s was a tremendous obstacle for baseball in general and for the Negro leagues in particular. Both Babe Ruth, the highest-paid major league player, and Kenesaw Mountain Landis, the commissioner of baseball, took cuts in pay along with everyone else. It was the only way to ensure baseball's survival. The Depression's effect on the chronically unstable Negro league teams was worse. Bill Foster recalled those days from a player's perspective: "The team couldn't pay us; it was the Depression and nobody was working. . . . The people couldn't go to the ball game, and our bosses promised us so much money but they didn't have it 'cause they weren't making it."[1] Most owners simply paid players a percentage of the gate receipts whenever they could get games.

It was left to another Fosteresque figure, Gus ("Big Red") Greenlee, to reestablish and reorganize the Negro National League. Greenlee, who first arrived in Pittsburgh about 1920, rose quickly in the Smoky City's gambling underworld. As the Depression deepened, Greenlee, headquartered at his Crawford Grille, was recognized by blacks as the numbers king of Pittsburgh. Already involved in the sporting scene as the owner of a stable of boxers that included John Henry Lewis, the world light-heavyweight champion, Greenlee sought to expand his investments in the sports world.

In 1931, with plenty of money but no real baseball experience, Greenlee set out to create the best black team in the nation. Focusing his financial strength on a small semipro outfit, the Crawford Colored Giants, he enjoyed immediate success by acquiring a promising young pitcher, Satchel Paige, from the disbanded Cleveland Cubs for $250. A love-hate relationship developed between player and owner because Paige constantly threatened to leave the Crawfords. Obtaining other good players posed no real problem. Cum Posey's Homestead Grays, based at Pittsburgh's Forbes Field, provided a ready source. In a short time, lured by the promise of financial stability and steady, lucrative salaries, a number of Posey's players jumped to Greenlee's team. Many old-timers believe Greenlee's original Pittsburgh Crawfords were one of the greatest black teams ever assembled. Besides Paige, the team included four other future Hall of Famers—player-manager Oscar Charleston, Judy Johnson, Cool Papa Bell, and the young slugger Josh Gibson.

Money was not Greenlee's only means of attracting players. Early in 1931 he undertook the construction of Greenlee Field. Attendance figures for blacks at the Pirates' Forbes Field across town convinced Greenlee that the black community would support a baseball diamond in its own neighborhood. At a cost of between $75,000 and $125,000, he built a 6,000-seat stadium to showcase his team. Since barnstorming was still the staple of black teams, he also purchased a twenty-two-passenger touring bus emblazoned with the team name on the side. With his stadium and a $70,000 bus with a cruising speed of sixty miles per hour,

The 1931 Homestead Grays. *Back row, left to right:* Cum Posey, owner; Bill Evans, shortstop; Jap Washington, first base; Ambrose Reid, outfield; Joe Williams, pitcher; Josh Gibson, catcher; George Scales, second base; Oscar Charleston, first base; Charley Walker, road secretary. *Front row:* George Britt, pitcher; Lefty Williams, pitcher; Jud Wilson, third base; Vic Harris, outfield; Ted Radcliffe, pitcher and catcher; Tex Barnett, catcher; Ted Page, outfield. *Courtesy of National Baseball Library, Cooperstown, N.Y.*

Greenlee had made it clear that his team was first class all the way.

Not since the days of Rube Foster and his Chicago American Giants, who traveled almost exclusively by Pullman cars and with five sets of uniforms, had black fans seen the likes of the Crawfords. Every black fan knew the Crawfords were the closest thing to major league. Their record of 99–36 in 1932 marked not only their success but the beginning of the golden era of the Negro leagues. Gus Greenlee had inherited Rube Foster's dream.

By 1933, despite the success of the Crawfords, their barnstorming schedule played havoc with Greenlee's investment. He decided that if black baseball was ever to become a paying proposition and regain the credibility lost in the immediate post-Foster years, what was needed was reorganization and resolute leadership. In his mind, this could be best achieved by resurrecting Foster's old league and by lowering ticket prices to attract more fans.

The New Negro National League

In January 1933, Greenlee put together his version of the Negro National League. It consisted of his Crawfords, Posey's Grays, the reorganized Indianapolis ABCs, the Detroit Stars, the Columbus Blue Birds, and the American Giants of Chicago. The league survived until 1948 when the integration of major league baseball led to its quiet demise.

Unlike Foster's earlier version, the new league had some financial stability due largely to a new breed of owner. Donn Rogosin, a historian of the Negro leagues, writes:

In this second phase of Negro league baseball, the numbers men played a dominating role. They were the

The 1934 Pittsburgh Crawfords, shown here at Yankee Stadium, were one of the all-time great black teams featuring five future Hall of Famers. *Left to right:* Jimmie Crutchfield, Bertrum Hunter, Roosevelt Davis, Leroy Morney, Chester Williams, W. G. Perkins, Clarence Palm, William Bell, James ("Cool Papa") Bell, Harry Kincannon, William J. ("Judy") Johnson, Leroy Matlock, Ted Page, Curtis Harris, Josh Gibson, Satchel Paige, Oscar Charleston. *Courtesy of National Baseball Library, Cooperstown, N.Y.*

Some of the star players from Gus Greenlee's Pittsburgh Crawfords standing beside the team's $70,000 bus. *Courtesy of National Baseball Library, Cooperstown, N.Y.*

small time, and not-so-small time gangsters of the black ghetto, and they were almost the only blacks with the money and inclination to subsidize black baseball. . . .

The numbers racketeers in the black community were black entrepreneurs and community leaders at the same time; they were men with money and they were expected to support the community. For many this obligation meant backing the black baseball team.[2]

Effa Manley, the wife of Abe Manley, who later owned the Newark Eagles, supported this view that status and pleasure, not profit, were the motives for ownership.[3] The search for legitimacy, then, led such men as Abe Manley, a retired gambler, Rufus ("Sonny Man") Jackson, described by Time as a "jukebox impresario,"[4] and Allessandro Pompez, who turned state's evidence in New York state rackets hearings,[5] to invest in the new venture and provide a measure of stability. Because of such ownership, Branch Rickey, the man later responsible for integrating baseball, described the Negro leagues in the following manner: "They are not leagues and have no right to expect organized baseball to respect them. They have the semblance of a racket and operate for the best interest of certain individuals."[6]

In 1938, Greenlee's Negro National League was joined by the Negro American League, the brainchild of H. G. Hall, then owner of the Chicago American Giants. The Negro American League concentrated its franchises in the Midwest and South as the Negro National League became primarily an eastern circuit. While the heart of the Negro American League was to be in the ghettos of Chicago, Cleveland, Kansas City, and St. Louis, the important change was the recognition of southern black interest in the new league system. Periodically represented in the league were such teams as the Jacksonville Red Caps, the Atlanta Black Crackers, and the Memphis Red Sox. But the strongest and most consistently represented southern contingent was the Birmingham Black Barons. With the exception of the Black Barons, these southern teams were the weak sisters in a league dominated by the Kansas City Monarchs, who won five pennants in the first nine years.

Because it had teams in the South, where there was no major league competition, the Negro American League outlived the Negro National League. In 1948, when the Negro National League folded, the younger circuit absorbed what teams it could and staggered on until 1960, when it too became history.

Despite the good intentions and financial stability of the organizers in both leagues, little changed with regard to the perennial problems of black baseball. Raiding, scheduling difficulties, and lack of a central authority continued to plague professional black baseball.

Where the Rookies Came From

Since Negro league teams could not afford scouts, barnstorming tours provided not only income but a chance to look for new talent on the sandlots of semipro baseball.

In his book *Voices of the Great Black Baseball Leagues,* an oral history of the black baseball experience, John Holway interviewed seventeen former Negro league stars. Fourteen of these players had been born in, and played semipro ball in, the Sunbelt states before joining teams in the professional Negro leagues. This was not exceptional. Many black athletes were from the South or, like Josh Gibson and Cool Papa Bell, came from families that had moved north with many other blacks during and after World War I.

Many a Negro leaguer owed his first break to a successful day against a northern professional team. In 1916, twenty-year-old Jesse Hubbard pitched the Alexandria, Louisiana, Giants to a shutout victory over the Chicago American Giants. The next year, John Henry ("Pop") Lloyd, who had played on that Giants team and had taken over the helm of the Brooklyn Royal Giants, returned to Louisiana and signed Hubbard.

The situation was similar for North Carolina's Buck Leonard. After being laid off from his railroad job in 1932, he was playing for the Portsmouth, Virginia, Firefighters when he was signed by the Baltimore Stars.

Northern barnstorming tours also led to the signing of players. George Sweatt was signed by the Kansas City Monarchs from the Iola, Kansas, Gold Devils. Transplanted southerner Cool Papa Bell joined the St. Louis Stars from the East St. Louis Cubs in 1922. There existed a subtle sectional friction even among blacks, as Jake Stephens, longtime shortstop with the Grays and Crawfords, has noted:

[Southerners] lived a different life than we lived. We didn't even much associate with them off the ball field because they were what you'd call clowns. They didn't dress the way we dressed, they didn't have the same mannerisms, the same speech.

And you have this other problem with Southern boys, they've never been used to making money. Give them $150 a month, first thing you know they go all haywire, living on top of the world.[7]

Southern black colleges were another source of talent. Negro league clubs would play these college teams during spring training. Competition with the professionals was viewed by the colleges as not only athletically beneficial but sound public relations as well. It provided exposure for the generally small regional colleges in the nationally prominent black newspapers, which devoted extensive coverage to black collegiate sports. For the professional teams, the newspaper coverage kept the fans back home informed of their teams' progress while whetting their appetites for the upcoming season. Although few in number, college men dotted Negro league rosters. New Orleans University, Edward Waters College in Jacksonville (Florida), Clark College (Georgia), Livingstone College (North Carolina), Talladega College (Alabama), Bethune-Cookman College (Florida),

Benedict College (South Carolina), Sam Houston State University (Texas), and Howard University (Washington, D.C.) could all claim alumni on the rosters of professional black teams.

The most frequently traveled path to the Negro leagues was through the two best-known black semipro leagues, the Texas Negro League and the Southern Negro League. These in effect served as the minor leagues of black baseball. The Texas league was the better of the two organizations largely because less racial tension was found there than in the deep South. As a result, interracial games, which generally drew large crowds, were easier to book, and salaries were higher.[8] Where possible, teams like the San Antonio Black Aces and the Austin Black Senators used the well-maintained fields of the white Texas league. The Black Aces were a veritable fount of talent, sending such players as Raleigh ("Biz") Mackey, one of the greatest Negro league catchers, Smokey Joe Williams, a pitcher who many old-timers contend was better than Satchel Paige, and first baseman Bob ("Highpockets") Hudspeth on to distinguished careers in the professional black leagues.

Finally, a touch of cosmopolitanism was added to the Negro National League by a large contingent of Cuban players. As a charter member of the league and an integral part of it during its whole existence, the Cuban teams of Allessandro Pompez (the Cuban Stars and the New York Cubans) were led by some outstanding players and were always an excellent drawing card.

According to most old-timers, the premier Cuban player was Martin Dihigo. A future member of both the Mexican, the Cuban, and the United States Baseball Halls of Fame, Dihigo was undoubtedly the most versatile performer in a league of multitalented players. After breaking into

MARTIN DIHIGO
(EL MAESTRO)
LIGA MEXICANA 1937-44, 1946-47, 1950

INCOMPARABLE PELOTERO CUBANO QUE SE
DISTINGUIO EN TODAS LAS POSICIONES, PERO
SOBRE TODO COMO PITCHER. BATEADOR
FORMIDABLE PRIMERO EN LANZAR SIN HIT NI
CARRERA (1937) Y EN CONECTAR 6 HITS EN 6 VECES
(1938), CON EL AGUILA DE VERACRUZ POSEE LOS
RECORDS DE MEJOR PORCENTAJE GLOBAL (.676) EN
GANADOS Y PERDIDOS (119-57), Y DE CARRERAS
LIMPIAS (2.84), EN TODOS LOS TIEMPOS. BATEO
.317 EN SU CARRERA.

Martin Dihigo, the most versatile player ever to play in the Negro leagues, is a member of the Cuban, the Mexican, and United States Halls of Fame. This is his Mexican Salon de Fame plaque. In translation it reads: "An incomparable Cuban player who distinguished himself at all positions but above all as a pitcher. A formidable hitter. He was the first to pitch a no-hitter (1937) and the first to go 6 for 6 in a game (1938). Played for the Vera Cruz Eagles. He holds all-time records in percentage (.676) won and lost (119–57), and earned-run average (2.84). He hit .317 for his career." *Courtesy of National Baseball Library, Cooperstown, N.Y.*

baseball in 1923 with the New York Cubans, Dihigo played every position. Bill Yancey, a shortstop for the New York Black Yankees in the 1930s, said that he had "seen them all for the past fifty years and I still think Dihigo was in a class by himself. He'd pitch one day, play centerfield the next, and the next day he'd be at first base. Sometimes he even played two or three positions in a single game."[9]

Other Cubans of note were Christobel Torrienti, who provided the power for Rube Foster's baseball machine; José Mendez, an outstanding pitcher and manager in the 1920s; and Luis Tiant, Sr., who in 1947, at age forty-one, was instrumental in pitching the New York Cubans to a league championship.

FOUR

Life in the Negro Leagues

Obtaining an opportunity to try out for any professional team, black or white, was not difficult, but securing a permanent position was a different matter, particularly in the Negro leagues. Major league clubs carried about two dozen players, but in an effort to keep expenses at a minimum, black team rosters were generally maintained at fourteen to nineteen players. The 200 or so positions available on black teams were closely guarded by the incumbents, as Quincy Trouppe recalled: "The competition for the Negro league was stiff and there was a lot of jealousy. Some of the men were afraid you might beat them out of their position. So there were few ballplayers who extended a hand to me when I joined the team although when you made a mistake, they sure let you know about it."[1]

The career longevity of black pro players was phenomenal, which further complicated the efforts of aspiring rookies. For example, Cool Papa Bell was a long-established star by 1945 when, at age forty-two, he hit .373. The next year he retired after hitting an astounding .412! Future Hall of Famer John Henry ("Pop") Lloyd, considered by many to be the best shortstop ever to play in the Negro leagues, was an active player until he retired at age forty-seven, and Oscar

Charleston and Buck Leonard went Lloyd one better, both retiring when they were forty-eight.

Regardless of age and length of service, a high premium was placed on player durability and stamina. With roster limitations and an almost nonstop schedule of league and barnstorming games, older men like Lloyd and Leonard still had to play regularly, even if injured. Being out of the lineup meant no pay and possible replacement. Alonzo Boone, manager of the Cleveland Buckeyes in 1948, explained that the reputation of Negro leaguers for endurance was not myth but necessity: "Players had to be on their toes because there was always a bunch of guys hanging around waiting to take your job. If you got hurt, you stayed in the lineup."[2] Louis Santop, a catcher for Hilldale, reportedly caught a doubleheader with a broken thumb. He won the first game with a triple and the second with a home run.[3] Buck Leonard remembered getting a cut in Washington that required three stitches, but the team was leaving for Boston and New Hampshire so he left. Eventually, the injury healed itself. Larry ("Iron Man") Brown once caught 234 games in one year.[4] Few catchers could not boast of catching three games in a single day. Willie Mays, a Negro leaguer before joining the New York Giants in 1950, recalled an incident that typified the league's expectations for players. As a teenager with the Black Barons, he was hit by a pitch and lay waiting for sympathy. Manager Lorenzo ("Piper") Davis came out and asked if Mays could see first base. When the youth replied that he could, the manager told him to get on it.

Versatility was another important consideration in player selection. Again, roster limitations dictated that players play more than one position, be accomplished in a number of skills, and even coach along the baselines. Smokey Joe

Williams, one of the tragically ignored Negro league greats, recalled:

Most of my career my team carried between ten and twelve men on the entire squad. When I wasn't pitching, I had to play outfield. In those days there was no platoon system. You had to pitch everyone, lefties as well as righties, and you had to finish every game you started unless there was an emergency. We had no pinch hitters. Couldn't afford them on the payroll. Pitchers just had to learn to hit. I was awful as a hitter when I started, but I finished with a lifetime average of .345.[5]

Black baseball tradition abounds with such adaptable performers. Ted ("Double Duty") Radcliffe got his nickname because during doubleheaders he often saw "double duty," pitching the first game and catching the second, or vice versa. Bullet Joe Rogan established his reputation as a pitcher but was such a good hitter that he played the outfield and batted cleanup on off days. Dave Barnhill, who played for the New York Cubans and later pitched for the major league New York Giants, hurled every fourth day and played first base the other three.

Payday

It is difficult to know exactly how much players were paid. Salaries varied from individual to individual, and teams differed in their methods of pay. As might be expected, player paychecks fluctuated with the economy. During the 1920s, monthly salaries averaged about $230, but during the Depression-ridden 1930s they fell to about $170. Of course, the stars of the league who attracted fans to the stadiums were paid more. Satchel Paige made $350 a month in 1937, and in the early 1940s Josh Gibson was recognized as the highest-paid black player, with a salary estimated at $1,000 a month. Both players made considerably more money during barnstorming tours between and after regular league season games.

Salaries paid major leaguers were not public knowledge. However, based on information leaked to the press by players and managers, the average annual salary was probably about $5,000 to $6,000 in the 1920s and about $7,000 in the 1930s. This was well below the top salary of $80,000 that Babe Ruth received in 1930. Although most Negro leaguers were paid less than their white counterparts in the major leagues, they were much better off than their black contemporaries outside baseball. Furthermore, they played twelve months a year, so on an annual basis some made more than their major leaguer counterparts. The league gave players a chance for some financial security as well as prestige, respect, and public esteem. No player would give these up without a real fight.

Former Crawfords and Grays star Ted Page recounted for author John Holway his own rationale for putting up with the difficulties of baseball during the Depression years: "This is the way I had to keep from washing windows in a downtown store or sweeping the floors and these were the kinds of jobs out there for us. So it was better than washing windows for fifteen dollars a week or twelve dollars a week. That was the average salary in those days."[6]

Dodgers catcher and Hall of Famer Roy Campanella concurred with Page. "A Negro ballplayer, playing Negro ball in the States might not have lived like a king, but he didn't live bad either. . . . Playing ball was a way to beat that [slums], to move on to something better."[7]

Spring Training

Black pro players, like their white counterparts, spent the period from February to April in places like New Orleans, Houston, and Hot Springs, Arkansas. This period was especially important for Negro league teams that used the time to "scout" and recruit players. Spring training also gave teams an opportunity to renew connections and establish popularity with their southern fans. Most of the players had relatives there as well, and although the teams were based primarily in the North, they had a following of loyal southerners who followed their wins and losses through the black weekly newspapers.

The first barnstorming tour of the new season served as spring training. Lacking the financial resources of white players, black players played themselves into shape while building the teams' treasuries playing before fans who paid to watch their heroes perform. Buck Leonard of the Grays described the general regimen:

> We would leave here about the last of February and go to Daytona or Orlando, Florida, for spring training. . . . We would go down there and spring train about five or six days and then we started playin' the local teams around there in Florida. We'd go down to West Palm Beach, down to Miami, come back to Ft. Lauderdale and we'd go to Tampa and play the Tampa Pepsi-Cola Giants, and we'd go to Jacksonville and play the Red Caps. . . . Then we'd come up to Atlanta and play the Atlanta Black Crackers, then we'd play in one or two

Grays' slugger and Hall of Famer Buck Leonard, racing in vain, is about to be called out at first base. *Courtesy of National Baseball Library, Cooperstown, N.Y.*

towns around Atlanta. Then we'd go to Birmingham and play the Black Barons and we'd go to New Orleans and play a team called the Black Pelicans. . . . and we'd play like that all the way back. We'd get back to Washington, D.C., about the twenty-fifth of April and we'd always play one game in Griffith Stadium before our league started on May first.[8]

In an article in *Ebony* in June 1948, Jackie Robinson, by then a Brooklyn Dodger and a bona fide black hero, described his spring training with the Kansas City Monarchs. He arrived at the Houston camp on a Friday. Saturday it rained, and on Sunday, with no practice at all, the team began playing local opponents. While Robinson's case may have been an exception, Leonard's was the rule. Little teaching took place in league camps. Players learned the finer points of the game by playing. There was no extra work, no special coaches to work on techniques, and no concern about conditioning. Such things were considered lavish and strictly for white clubs with money. The only question anyone asked was could the man play.

Pitchers

Perhaps the best-known, most outspoken, and most flamboyant Negro league players were the pitchers; they held center stage every day, and they knew it. Such players as Smokey Joe Williams, Satchel Paige, Bullet Joe Rogan, Willie Foster, and Cannonball Dick Redding were at one time or another selected on all-time Negro league teams. Their skills were legendary.

Nat Rogers, an outfielder with the Chicago American Giants, said of Willie Foster: "In spring training, you know how he'd get his control? Set two bats about a foot apart and throw right between them."[9] Outfielder Clint Thomas asserted that the New York Yankees hired Dick Redding to pitch batting practice to a young Lou Gehrig, who was attending Columbia.[10] Satchel Paige's pregame warmup saw him take a cigarette, discard the tobacco, and use the paper as a plate. Such stars usually played only against Negro league competition or against the white major leaguers in postseason tours. "We had pitchers that would pitch in league games and mediocre pitchers that we used against white semipro teams," recalled Buck Leonard.[11]

Despite their recognized skills, pitchers were not above using intimidation or tricky baseball to win. George Jefferson of the Cleveland Buckeyes explained the pitcher-hitter confrontation: "A pitcher had to get in shape to survive. Teams carried very few relievers, so you knew most of the time you would be going the distance. People like Buck Leonard and Piper Davis never gave you a break. When you went out there you had better be ready. Guys had reputations they were trying to protect and believe me, they did."[12]

Hitters would do anything to get on base, as infielder and Hall of Famer Judy Johnson confessed: "Me being a right handed batter, I would have the left sleeve a little baggier than my right and then I'd lean and just let the ball tick my sleeve or I'd puff my shirt in front and let the ball tick me there."[13]

The beanball and pitches thrown at a batter's body were a way of life, as Newark Eagles' pitcher Leon Day reported: "Most of the time it was understood. It was an unwritten code. 'You dig a hole on me in the box; I'll knock you down.' Hitters knew it." Remembering Smokey Joe Williams, Frank Forbes said:

> Joe was a real cutey. Joe had a lot of control. I mean like he'd cut your throat up here with a fast ball inside and then come down on the outside corner on the knees with the next one. He'd move a guy out of the box see? I'd tell him "move 'em around," he knew what I meant. You've got to be a hell of a hitter to dig in on him, especially if you take a full cut at the ball. He'd cut you down. Then you're not in there so firm. Then the next pitch he comes outside on you, you can't get it.[14]

Hitters were not entirely at the mercy of pitchers. Vic Harris, a great base runner and fine manager, described the means of retaliation most often employed: "The pitcher would throw at your head. So you'd have to drag the ball so the first baseman would have to field it and the pitcher would cover. That's when you get him back—step on his foot."[15]

Bill Drake, a pitcher known for his willingness to throw at a hitter, refused to play winter ball in Cuba because he felt some of his victims would be laying for him.[16]

Negro league pitchers were notorious for doctoring the ball to get that little extra edge on the batters. Cool Papa Bell reminisced: "In our league they threw the spitter, the screw ball, the emery ball, shine ball—that means Vaseline ball: there was so much Vaseline on it, it made you blink your eyes on a sunny day. Then they threw the mud ball—the mud on its seams made it sink. The emery ball would break either up or down, but if a sidearmer threw it and didn't know what he was doing, it could sail right into a hitter."[17]

Roy Campanella offered a similar view and discussed the problems a catcher had handing such pitches:

Anything went in the Negro National League. Spit-balls, shine balls, emery balls; pitchers used any and all of them. They nicked and moistened and treated the ball to make it flutter and spin, dip and break. Not only were there no rules against it, there weren't enough spare baseballs around to substitute clean unmarked ones for the damaged ones, like they do in the big leagues. I was never sure what a ball would do once it left the pitcher's hand, even when he threw what I called for. A man could get hurt catching in the col-ored league.[18]

Bill Harvey used a phonograph needle. "What you'd do was jam a needle in the laces and then rub some dirt over it. Then, depending how you'd grip the ball, you could make it go up, down, or out."[19] Chet Brewer told Donn Rogosin about his unique way to doctor a ball: "I liked to pitch when [Oscar] Charleston was playing first base. He was so strong, when you threw him a new ball to rub up he could just take it in his hands and open up a seam on it."[20] To put an end to Brewer's antics in one game, manager Judy Johnson, after protesting to the umpires and getting no satisfaction, ordered Joe Williams to hit the first batter of the inning. When the Monarchs complained, Johnson just said the ball was so worked over that his pitcher could not be blamed for his lack of control.[21]

On the Base Paths

While getting on base was an achievement, it did not mean the end of a batter's harassment. Shortstop Dobie Moore would grab the belt of a runner rounding second or third just enough to throw him off stride. This was often the difference in a close play at third or home plate.[22] Jake Stephens, another shortstop, happily remembered his version of the old hidden ball trick: "I used to stand behind the runner with the ball in my glove, get him off guard in conversation: 'Heh, man you sure are hitting the ball. . . . Excuse me, let me straighten the base,' and he'd step off. Then you show him the ball. And the best part is always say 'Excuse me' just before you put the ball on him."[23]

Such antics were relatively harmless, but there was also a darker side for the base runner. Jelly Gardner's thoughts were those of a number of old-time players: "When you got on first it was pretty rough going. Infielders would come down on your legs, spike the base runner. You had to duck those throws on double plays, you had to duck the ball. They'd throw it at you. You needed hats like they got now at that time. All the infielders wore shin guards like a catcher—and they needed them."[24]

In 1942, Willie Wells, after a serious beaning, became the first player to wear a batting helmet. Wells, recovering from a concussion, could not afford to miss any more games so he borrowed a hard hat from a construction worker and wore it to the plate. The other players thought he was crazy.

On the Field

Defensive players faced danger too. Beyond a doubt, infield positions were the most dangerous places on the diamond. More than one infielder observed players in the dugout sharpening their spikes, or heard threats shouted in their direction. A Negro league runner never slid on his stomach, hands reaching for the bag; that was an open invitation for a spiking by a defensive player covering the bag. Instead runners always slid with their spikes up. Players developed reputations as slashing base runners. Julio Rojo of the New York Cubans was known as "the Cuban Cutter." Catchers seemed to get a great deal of abuse, as Jake Stephens recalled: "[Suppose the team at bat is a] couple runs ahead and the ball is hit to left field, we used to slow up when we went around third, make the outfield throw so we could jump on the catcher. They'd slow up one or two steps, just to make it close at home plate."[25]

Catcher Frank Duncan in responding to the question, "Who was the toughest runner?" replied: "If I didn't get the ball in time all of them were tough. . . . Couldn't leave your post, had to stay there and they're trying to cut you. . . . In them days they didn't get out of your way. If you were in the way of that base they were going to try to move you."[26]

Reprisal was a way of life in the league, and second baseman Newt Allen told of one such incident:

See that scar on my shin? Eighteen stitches in that. I got it from the third baseman of the American Giants by the name of Dave Malarcher. I had him out by about ten feet and was going to tag him, when he came in with one foot high. I was out quite a while. It took me three years to repay him, but they say vengeance is sweet. One day we were leading by two runs, he was on first, and I took the throw at second for a double play. Well, instead of throwing to first, I threw straight at Malarcher charging into second. I hit him right in the forehead, just enough under his cap bill to keep from breaking his nose. Hurt him pretty bad. He was out of the ball game for three days. The next time he was on first and rounding second to go to third, I could have thrown the ball over his head and gotten him out, but it was just one of those "evil spirit" days. I cut down on him overhanded and hit him right in the back of the head. That hurt him pretty bad too, but that's the way they played the game then. But he never slid into me with his spikes up again.[27]

There were other ways to defend oneself, as Allen elaborated:

Years later I learned that if they jump high, watch the leg that's in the air. If he's going to try to spike with it, step aside and hook it with your arm. . . . You want to hook your arm just past his shoes and pull. I could throw a man ten feet and break his neck almost. You do that to one or two bad sliders and you don't have any trouble out of the rest. Or hit two or three of them coming into second base in the chest with the ball— next time they'll run right out of the base path.[28]

As might be expected, such aggressiveness led to fights. One of the biggest rumbles in league history was between the Monarchs and the Chicago American Giants. Catcher Frank Duncan tried to score from second on a single. Jelly Gardner threw the ball to the plate on one hop, and John Hines, the American Giants' catcher, simply waited for the obvious out. Duncan had other ideas and jumped at Hines and cut him. Both benches and the stands emptied before the Chicago police arrived to restore order. League officials understandably tried to minimize such fights, not only for the integrity of the black game but for the hope of eventual integration as well. Othello Renfroe reported: "I tell you just about everybody would fight. Very seldom you played a ball game—a really close ball game, two teams fighting for a pennant or for second place or something— you didn't have a fight. The game was just that heated. The manager didn't want you out there if you didn't have some fight in you. You'd fight your own teammates if they were loafing."[29]

The Men in Blue

Certainly some of the blame for the disregard of the rules and poor conduct by players must fall on the umpires who often failed to control the game objectively. The general opinion of most ex-Negro leaguers was that the umpiring was universally poor. Consider Cool Papa Bell's recollection: "We didn't have the umpires we should have had. It wasn't that they couldn't umpire, but, sometimes an umpire would favor the home team; sometimes they were old ballplayers who had played with this team."[30]

Even the redoubtable Rube Foster wrote: "To be an official umpire the first great step for the umpire is to study

Arguments were an occupational hazard for umpires in all leagues, black and white. Hall of Famer Monte Irvin of the Newark Eagles looks on in dismay as an opponent from the Philadelphia Stars tries to make a point with the home plate umpire. *Courtesy of Larry Lester/Negro Leagues Baseball Museum, Inc.*

the disposition and temperament of players with whom he comes in contact; to be a good judge of human nature, to know baseball rules, their interpretation, and to be HONEST and SQUARE. These qualifications are sadly missing in the umpires I have seen perform."[31]

Poor umpiring was the result of a number of factors. In the first place, there was no association of umpires. And umpires received no support from the league. For example, in one game between the Lincoln Giants and the Bacharach Giants, third baseman Oliver Marcelle got into an argument and was ejected. The offender was slow leaving the field, and the umpire called a forfeit in favor of Bacharach. Lincoln owner James Keenan reversed the umpire's decision, and play continued.[32] Even when the league began assigning umpires they were only for home plate. Base umpires were selected by the home team. Pitcher Bill Drake remembered playing games where a man from the stands was called on to umpire.[33]

This lack of professionalism did not create respect, and players argued, cursed, and sometimes pushed and shoved or hit umpires in their anger over a call. Jud ("Boojum") Wilson was a notorious umpire baiter and at times in his career chased umpires with a bat, threw water on them, and fought with them.

Despite the generally poor state of umpiring in the Negro leagues, one conscientious umpire in the league who wanted to get a better view of the plate was probably the first man to invent and use an inside chest protector. John Craig placed sponges between two flattened sheets of cardboard, taped the sheets together, and wore the protector inside his coat, enabling him to see the plate better from over the catcher's shoulder.

The All-star Game

The high point of the Negro league season was the East-West All-star Game. The game, conceived by Gus Greenlee, pitted the stars of the National League's eastern division against their western counterparts. After 1937, the Negro American League represented the West and the National League the East. When the National League folded in 1948, the game returned to the divisional format in the surviving Negro American League until it was abolished in 1950 for financial reasons.

The game's greatest stars gathered annually in August for this game amid a carnival atmosphere. As the city with

The East-West All-star Game brought the best players in the Negro leagues together in a competition usually held in Chicago. This is the 1939 East team. *Standing, from left to right:* Buck Leonard, first base; Willie Wells, shortstop; Fern Fernandes, catcher; Sammy Hughes, second base; George Scales, second base; Mule Suttles, left field; Pat Patterson, third base; Josh Gibson, catcher; Bill Wright, right field; Roy Partlow, pitcher. *Kneeling:* Bill Byrd, pitcher; Leon Day, pitcher; Bill Holland, pitcher; Condo Lopez, center field; Goose Curry, outfield; Red Parnell, left field. *Courtesy of National Baseball Library, Cooperstown, N.Y.*

the strongest fan support in the league and the hub of the midwestern black community, Chicago was the undisputed home of the East-West game. The players were chosen by a vote of the fans conducted by the two major black newspapers, the *Chicago Defender* and the *Pittsburgh Courier.* As might be expected, teams from the large cities, where there were lots of voting fans, sent the most players to the game.

The average attendance at the late-season classic was 38,274; a record crowd for this event—51,723—saw the game in 1943. The contest not only gave the teams exposure, since this was the one Negro league event covered by the white media, but also offered a partial solution for the league's financial problems. Horace G. Hall, owner of the

Chicago American Giants, said, "The East-West game helped us out of the hole. It was divided [among all teams], but it helped us to pay our players and get ready for another season."[34]

More than one ex-player, including Dave Malarcher, Jack Marshall, and Frank Forbes, has said that the success of the East-West game was the real reason baseball was finally integrated. Based on East-West attendance figures, white owners realized that the black community was a virtually untapped reservoir of support for their clubs. They were aware also that it would be necessary to sign black players to attract the black fans who attended the East-West game. Such ex-players steadfastly assert it was not for humanitarian reasons that men like Branch Rickey finally integrated baseball, but for the money the black community would spend to see its heroes playing in the major leagues.

A world series between winners of the Negro National and American Leagues, when both leagues existed, or between division winners of the Negro National League, officially ended the season, but it never received the notoriety of the all-star game. Baseball historian Donn Rogosin offers a very plausible reason: "The black population was unable to support a seven- or nine-game series over a short period. The black population was not big enough. The black fan's . . . income was not large enough, nor his leisure time extensive enough."[35]

Winter Ball

Cold weather signaled the start of another phase of life for black players. Winter found players and teams searching the warmer climate of the Sunbelt for games that would provide an income until the following spring.

Catcher Quincy Trouppe about to tag a sliding Monte Irvin in the 1947 East-West game. *From the photo archives of Refocus Films.*

Early in the century, some teams spent the winter working and playing at the luxury hotels of Palm Beach, Florida. Fittingly, it was Rube Foster who established the concept of year-round baseball for black players. Each year, Rube brought his Chicago American Giants to the Poiciana Hotel as a rival for the Eastern League New York Lincoln Giants, who wintered at the Breakers Hotel.

This was the closest thing black players had to an off season. They were paid a modest salary by the hotel management and received room and board in nearby segregated quarters. In return, the athletes practiced and played two games a week for the entertainment of the guests. Games were played on a makeshift diamond in the center of a golf course between the two hotels. Often the guests tipped players for good plays. Since the hotels required no other duties, the players had lots of free time. Dave Malarcher painted pictures on coconuts and sold them as souvenirs to the guests. Other players enjoyed the sun and hobnobbing with the nation's wealthy.[36] When the Breakers burned in 1924, black players followed the sun to other places.

In the 1920s, a growing black population along the west coast wanted to see their heroes play; Negro leaguers were more than obliging. Winter league play in California varied. Usually there was one black team in a four-team circuit. At first, this was a club imported from the East, such as the Brooklyn Royal Giants or the New York Lincoln Giants. In time, and especially at the height of the league's fortunes, the black representative evolved into an all-star team like the Los Angeles Black White Sox. Other members were industrial teams, like the White Kings Soap Company or the Shell Oil nine from Long Beach, California, suitably fortified with white minor and major leaguers. The Pacific Coast League, a well-respected minor league operation, usually entered its all-star team as well. The games were highly publicized, and the pay was always good.

The Latin Connection

As a respite from barnstorming, the most sought after positions in the winter were in the tropical leagues, especially Cuba, Mexico, Puerto Rico, and Venezuela. These leagues were popular with both black and white players from the

United States because travel was minimal and teams played only about three games a week. There was time to rest and recuperate from the long northern season.

The winter tropical leagues exploded the myth that blacks and whites could not play together. Integration was the way of life both on and off the field in these countries. Furthermore, the black American players were idolized and treated with respect by the appreciative Latins. Pitcher Bill Byrd of the Columbus Blue Birds and Baltimore Elite Giants remarked: "Down there you were treated better. . . . They'd pay your way down, get you an apartment, and pay you pretty well. . . . They would roll out the red carpet for you."[37]

In an interview with Wendell Smith of the *Pittsburgh Courier,* Newark shortstop Willie Wells gave eloquent testimony to the importance of this acceptance factor to the American black:

> *Not only do I get more money playing here, but I live like a king. . . . In the first place, I am not faced with the racial problem in Mexico. . . . When I travel with Vera Cruz we live in the best hotels, we eat in the best restaurants, and can go any place we care to. You know as well as other Negroes that we don't enjoy such privileges in the United States. We stay in any kind of hotel, far from the best, and eat only where we know we will be accepted. Until recently, Negro players in the United States had to go all over the country in buses, while in Mexico we've always traveled in trains. . . . We have everything first class here, plus the fact that the people here are much more considerate than the American baseball fan. I mean that we are heroes here, and not just ballplayers. . . . I've found freedom and democracy here, something I never*

found in the United States. I was branded a Negro in
the States and had to act accordingly. Every thing I
did, including playing ball, was regulated by my color.
Well, here in Mexico, I am a man. I can go as far in
baseball as I am capable of going. I can live where I
please and will encounter no restrictions of any kind
because of my race.[38]

There were other tangible recognitions too. The year his team won the Venezuelan championship, Quincy Trouppe was awarded the title honorary mayor of the city of Caguas.[39] To mark Josh Gibson's home runs, Latin fans hung banners from the trees. Martin Dihigo was elected to the Mexican Baseball Hall of Fame in 1964, a full thirteen years prior to his enshrinement at Cooperstown. A statue of Dihigo, one of the most versatile players of all time, now stands in the Temple of Baseball Immortals in Monterey, Mexico. A stone marker commemorating the storied feats of Josh Gibson stands in San Juan, Puerto Rico, and according to Willie Wells, there was a plaque in Havana's Tropical Park recalling one of Mule Suttles's homers until it was removed by order of Fidel Castro.[40] It is indeed ironic that such great athletes had to go so far to receive the recognition they so richly deserved.

Playing in the tropics was financially rewarding for black players. Othello Renfroe remembered: "We also made money in Latin America. . . . They'd pay a guy $1,000 a month, all expenses, no income tax. A guy could go down there and save $3,000 to $4,000."[41] Ted ("Double Duty") Radcliffe made $750 a month during one stint in the Mexican League.[42]

But all was not idyllic. Satchel Paige had the usual complaints about the food and the water, and there were other problems of adjustment. Lenny Pearson's comments indicate that while players liked Puerto Rico, they were anxious to get home: "Most of us will be glad when it's over, not that we dislike it or anything but it is so lonely. The people here are very nice. They try in every way to make us contented and happy, but we can't speak their language and they are hard to understand."[43]

Even the game was different. The Latins liked power baseball. They didn't care for the strategic black game. Cool Papa Bell was roundly booed when he bunted. If he beat out the bunt, fans considered it an error.[44] And playing conditions sometimes left something to be desired. In his autobiography *Maybe I'll Pitch Forever,* Satchel Paige recalled an incident in Puerto Rico. While playing the outfield, he noticed an iron "pipe" by the fence. When the next batter hit a liner that landed near the pipe, Paige saw the pipe move as he reached for the ball. The pipe was a boa constrictor.[45]

Although most players enjoyed their trips to the tropics, they looked forward to spring and a return to their homes and families. Few stayed on, because the best regular competition was stateside. By February, most players returned to their respective clubs to resume league play and life on the road.

FIVE

Barnstorming with the Negro Leaguers

No aspect of Negro league baseball contributed more to the legend of the league than barnstorming tours in which teams traveled from town to town to play the local talent. It was in the baseball-starved hinterland of America that money could be made; it was there that black teams sought financial solvency. For white major leaguers, barnstorming was done only after the regular season as a way of supplementing salaries. For black teams it was done throughout the year and was often their major source of income.

Professional Negro league baseball teams played three types of games. They played other teams in their league, they played local semipro teams, and they played games solely to entertain, showcasing skills comparable to those of today's Harlem Globetrotters in basketball. In these games the score was unimportant. The "opposition" consisted of teams such as the Zulu Giants, whose uniforms were imported Hawaiian grass skirts; the Indianapolis Clowns, who, true to their name, wore clown makeup and colorful uniforms; and other teams with a theatrical bent.

Although Negro league players took their profession seriously, they enjoyed entertaining the fans, and owners used a variety of tactics to increase ticket sales. At one time, the Toledo Crawfords traveled with Olympic sprinter Jesse Owens, who would race fans or horses before the game. He would usually give fans a ten-yard head start and take a similar lead himself against horses. On at least one occasion, he raced a horse from the same starting line and won. He refused, however, to take on Cool Papa Bell in a race around the base paths.

Satchel Paige used to say that Bell was so fast he could flick the light switch and get into bed before the room went dark. Everyone thought this to be just another one of Satchel's colorful comparisons until the soft-spoken Bell told his version. It seems that while Bell and Paige were roommates on a road trip, Bell discovered that there was a poor connection in the light switch for their room in the run-down hotel where they were staying. He decided to have some fun. Satchel returned later that evening and said he was tired and was going to bed. Bell said, "You know Satchel, I'm so fast I can beat the light out!" With that, he flipped the switch and leapt into bed before the light went out.

There was an aspect of levity in black baseball that was never duplicated in the major leagues. Fans arrived early to watch the pregame shows. Early on, black players became famous for what was called "shadow ball." This was simply playing the game without a ball, an elaborate pantomime complete with diving catches, acrobatic leaps, and the speed that black baseball was famous for. Other activities included home run–hitting and throwing contests. One throwing contest that lives on in Negro league lore involved Martin Dihigo and a jai alai player. In attempting to throw a ball into the centerfield bleachers from home plate, the jai alai player cleared the fence on a bounce. Dihigo threw a bullet that cleared the fence and went into the bleachers on the fly.[1]

Cool Papa Bell is held up at third base by Grays' manager, Candy Jim Taylor, in a game played in 1947 at Griffith Stadium, Washington, D.C. *Courtesy of National Baseball Library, Cooperstown, N.Y.*

Depending on the score, the fans' reaction to pregame activities, and spectator interest, the hijinks might continue during the game. A home run hitter would trot around the bases in reverse order; a low strike call by the umpire might lead a player to hit while on his knees; a ball hit to third would be thrown to each infielder before making the putout at first. Pepper Bassett of the New Orleans Crescent Stars would sometimes catch while sitting in a rocking chair behind home plate. Former Monarchs catcher Frank Duncan nostalgically summarized the feelings of a number of players in those days: "We would give the people our very best and we wanted to be their friends. I never heard an unkind word and we found an awful lot of nice people. . . . We liked playing in our own little American towns best. We loved the kids and we liked the folks. Those were great wonderful days."[2]

Game Time

The number of league games, in a season that began in May and extended through September, varied with the year, the club, and available stadium dates. About fifty games were standard. Of course, league games were supplemented by the profitable barnstorming schedule. The two combined would tax even the most accomplished and dedicated performer. As an example, one need look at only a portion of the 1932 Pittsburgh Crawford schedule. After April 2nd until July 21st, the Craws played ninety-four games in one hundred nine days. There were thirteen rainouts and only two open days. Their bus logged 17,000 miles.[3] The big days for league play were Saturday and Sunday. Most teams played a doubleheader on Sunday. After lights made night games possible, they would often play a night game *after* a doubleheader. Owners wanted to make the most of the rental fees they paid for major league parks.

Playing in the Negro leagues was not for the faint-hearted. It was demanding and intense, a no-holds-barred proposition, and it could be both dangerous and career threatening.

The Schedule and the Competition

Today's major league teams play an average of six games each week. If they're on the road, which is true for about three months each season, they travel (usually by plane) twice during the week. Such a schedule would have seemed like heaven to those who barnstormed with a Negro league team. In an interview with Atlanta radio station WRFG, James ("Gabby") Kemp, playing manager of the Atlanta Black Crackers, explained the usual routine: "We would barnstorm three days and we would meet the league team in a city on a Friday night, play that Friday night in the big city and play outside the city in another town about, maybe in a range of well, 120, well 200 miles. We'd play there and get back to play a double header in that big town. That would make up a total of seven to eight to ten games a week."[4]

Understandably, the quality of nonleague competition was irregular. White semipro teams like the Paterson (New Jersey) Silk Sox, the Lancaster (Pennsylvania) Red Roses, the West Haven (Connecticut) Sailors, and the Brooklyn (New York) Bushwicks flourished from playing the Philadelphia and New York Negro League entries and provided a challenge for the seasoned pros. In fact, one report stated that the Bushwicks, a group of white players with major league talent who played mostly Negro league opponents, actually outdrew the hapless St. Louis Browns of the (white) American League in 1946. Local teams like these were occasionally competitive, especially around large cities where the security of a regular job kept a number of quality players at home.

Reporting on the exploits of black greats Dick Redding and Joe Williams, the New London, Connecticut, daily paper expressed the sentiments of a number of humbled local players aspiring to professional status: "New London was helpless in Redding's hand, Redding hasn't Williams' control, but he has more steam throwing a ball that goes at a terrific speed. Both Williams and Redding, were they blondes instead of pronounced brunettes, would be wearing major league uniforms."[5]

Beating the local favorites handily could be costly. It might mean one less game the next season, so black teams would often give away a run or two. For example, in one

Smokey Joe Williams *(left)* and Cannonball Dick Redding, two of baseball's greatest pitchers. Neither has yet been recognized by the Hall of Fame. *Courtesy of Larry Lester/Negro Leagues Baseball Museum, Inc.*

game the Pittsburgh Crawfords were leading a U.S. Marine Corps team 12–0 in the bottom of the ninth. Satchel Paige and battery mate Josh Gibson, in a patriotic moment, decided to give the leathernecks a run. With the corps captain at bat, Paige served up a good pitch. The batter chopped the ball in front of Gibson, who promptly overthrew first base by about thirty feet. By the time the first baseman got the ball, the marine was around third and coming home. The relay bounced off Gibson's chest protector, and the catcher could only grin and say, "I had a feeling you were gonna be a hero."[6]

The Nomadic Life of Black Baseball

After his selection to the Hall of Fame, Satchel Paige said, "I had more fun and seen more places with less money than if I was Rockefeller."[7] But for most Negro league players, there was no glamour in the nomadic life. When teams like the Chicago American Giants began a barnstorming tour, they usually traveled by train just like their major league counterparts. However, as the stops became more frequent, the towns more obscure, and train connections more difficult, they switched to buses or cars. More often than not, it was the discomfort of constant travel rather than a decline in skills that led players to retire.

Spotswood Poles, Judy Johnson, and Dave Malarcher were all victims of the demanding traveling life-style. Johnson remembered, "It seemed like we were always riding, like we traveled from one end of the world to the other."[8] Not even the gas-rationing restrictions of World War II put a dent in the teams' tour schedules, because league clubs were exempted. The work they did was praised by the federal government for its entertainment value. George Jefferson of the Cleveland Buckeyes reminisced: "Don't get the idea that baseball was all fun and games for us. We played a lot of cards and dice to break the monotony of long bus rides. You saw more trees and bushes than you ever thought existed."[9]

Monte Irvin, a Negro league veteran who was a star for the New York Giants and was selected to the Hall of Fame,

enjoyed the three- or four-day stays in a city that character-
ized travel in the white major leagues. He reflected with some
bitterness on the contrasting style of travel in the Negro
leagues: "The reason they [the black leagues] ended as
soon as they did was due to mismanagement and greedi-
ness. The scheduling was so hectic that it contributed to the
shortening of many careers. Can you imagine playing in
Kansas City one night, the next night playing in Birmingham,
the next night in St. Louis, the next day a double header in
Newark, the next evening you find yourself in New York, and
the next night in Boston?"[10]

Irvin was not exaggerating; such marathons were regular fare for black professional ball players. Bill Harvey
recalled:

> We'd start out in Houston, then go on to Little Rock,
> Arkansas, and play that night. From there, we'd go to
> Memphis, Tennessee, play there and move on to Nash-
> ville and then Knoxville. Then we'd go to Asheville,
> North Carolina, play there and go to Baltimore, Phila-
> delphia, and then spend two weeks in New York. From
> New York we'd head up to Boston, then over to Buffalo,
> Cleveland, and Detroit. Then we'd head back south. All
> that time, of course, you didn't get to bed. One guy'd
> be drowsing on another guy's shoulder. I wasn't much
> of a sleeper though. I'd ride that bus at night and just
> look out the window at the lights.[11]

Hall of Famer Judy Johnson remembered the physical
hardships an eight-hundred-mile jaunt imposed after a
doubleheader in Chicago: "Right after the game we had a
meal, and then we started out for Philadelphia. We had our
bus all packed before the game. And we rode all the way to

Philadelphia without sleeping except for naps on the bus. The only thing we had to eat was sandwiches and pop. And when we got to Philadelphia, my ankles were swollen ten inches wide. We got in Tuesday noon and played a double-header that afternoon."[12]

In order to meet such widely separated commitments, speed was of the essence and for some teams, like the Homestead Grays, a bus moved too slowly, so touring cars were substituted. "We had to make 100 miles every two hours, and if you got a car that ran fifty-five miles per hour you were moving. There weren't any turnpikes either. All we had were those little bitty two-lane roads and some of them weren't any better than dirt roads. Today, we'd be doing eighty-five to ninety and we'd probably all end up singing with the angels."[13]

Clearly, travel was a risky proposition and accidents were just one more adversity to overcome. Willie Grace of the Cleveland Buckeyes recalled that in 1946, the team bus turned over three times exiting the Pennsylvania Turnpike on the way to Washington.[14] Judy Johnson remembered a race to Shreveport, Louisiana, when driver Oscar Charleston's car suffered a blowout and went off the road, spewing players along the roadside gully. Fortunately, there were no injuries, but Charleston emerged from the wreckage with a piece of steering wheel in each hand.[15] Sadly, not all mishaps were so injury free. In 1942, two Jacksonville Red Cap players were killed while fixing a flat tire. The Birmingham Black Barons carried the Homestead Grays to the limit in the 1945 Negro World Series only to see a car wreck ruin their chances in the deciding game. The second baseman was "broke all to pieces," the third baseman sustained a head injury, one of the catchers hurt his arm, and a utility infielder injured his leg.[16]

A barnstorming team poses beside its "chariot." Seen here is Kansas City Monarchs' owner J. L. Wilkinson and his team in the midst of a Canadian tour. Note the bearded white faces. They were players from the House of David, a white team that also spent much of its time on the road. *Courtesy of Larry Lester/Negro Leagues Baseball Museum, Inc.*

Business Tricks of the Game

Booking barnstorming games to provide income between league contests wasn't hard; getting paid required financial shrewdness. While league games were played on a percentage basis, barnstorming contests were negotiated. One player explained the usual business logic:

> *When a white ball club wrote and asked us for a game, they might offer a $500 guarantee. Well if they offered a guarantee, you won't accept that; you want a percentage. But if they say they will give you sixty percent of the gate, then you ask for a guarantee. Simple as that because when they want to give you a big guarantee they know they're going to make it. And when they're not sure they're going to make it, they want you to take a percentage, so you want a guarantee.*[17]

A game was often followed by money problems. James ("Gabby") Kemp of the Black Crackers recounted the bittersweet system of "deducts," which deducted from earnings all manner of unforeseen costs:

When we'd go to a city barnstorming that was where the "deducts" got you. The person in the city in which we were playing would be in with the man that managed the ball park and would . . . deduct from the total we had made. He'd deduct for the umpire, he would deduct for the ball park, and he would sometimes deduct for the police service. . . . Sometimes we didn't know whether he was putting the bite on us for maybe five or ten percent or whether he was honest, but we accepted whatever was given to us as the gate receipts.[18]

To combat this, the Black Crackers relied on the wife of owner John Hardin, Mrs. Billie Hardin, who often traveled with the team. According to Kemp:

Mrs. Hardin would travel with the ball club to those towns in which the gate was to be ten to twenty thousand people, and she learned the tricks that they'd use. She'd be there so the "ducts" wouldn't get us and she'd be there when they'd check that money out and when those men got up and started "ducting," Mrs. Hardin would "duct" right along with them. . . . Consequently, they stopped "ducting" on the Black Crackers because Mrs. Hardin got hip to the jive they were puttin' out with the "ducts."[19]

They're Here! They're Here!

Such money squabbles seldom dimmed the small-town festivities that heralded the arrival of a touring black team. To promote the upcoming game, there would be parades with the teams in uniform, the local band, and a traveling minstrel show, or black musicians hired to play at the postgame dance. Local businessmen might give half-day holidays and barbecues at the local ball park. James ("Red") Moore reflected on those times: "People were glad to see the team coming to town. . . . A lot of people (both black and white) . . . loved the Atlanta Black Crackers. They would have signs showing the players. . . . Made you feel real proud, you know, having your name on a big picture."[20]

In a number of rural areas, curiosity alone boosted attendance. Judy Johnson recalled one such experience in the coal fields of Pennsylvania: "No Negroes lived up in the hard coal regions. No Negroes were up there at all. We were regular freaks. When we played in one town we went for dinner and kids were around the front of the hotel just as though it was a circus or something. And if you walked up to some of those kids they would run away from you. They had never seen a Negro before."[21]

On the Road with Jim Crow

The confines of league play within major American cities with large black populations provided some shelter from the humiliating segregation of society. But during barnstorming tours, along the less-traveled roads of rural America, prejudice was glaringly evident. It was an ever-present companion of the black players. Years later, Buck Leonard said it best: "You had to continue to realize you were black. It stayed on your mind all the time. There were certain places you couldn't go and things you couldn't do."[22]

While white major league teams slept in the best hotels and enjoyed good food, black clubs found the simplest amenities of life on the road—lodging and food—difficult to come by. In urban areas with a large black population there was little problem with housing, but in smaller towns, players were forced to accept whatever could be found. Usually they were split into small groups and slept in rooming houses, private black homes, the YMCA, or even the local jails. Segregation relegated black players to second-class hotels that served as constant reminders of their social position. Buck Leonard remembered places so infested with bedbugs that players put newspapers between the mattresses and the sheets.[23] Mrs. Billie Hardin recalled a particularly bad hotel in which pieces of old sheets served as wash cloths.[24]

Frequently, black players had to contend with petty harassment from the local authorities. Judy Johnson recounted one such incident:

In Nashville when I was managing the Grays, this one policeman made us get off the street because he didn't like the way we looked. We always dressed nice, like professional people, and when we traveled, we wore white knickers and these little blue tams. One morning five or six of us went up town to do some shopping, and this white officer came over to us and said, "Say, you niggers go back where you belong and put on some decent clothes. Don't y'all come up town looking like that no more."[25]

Johnson faced a somewhat similar situation when he was returning with teammates from winter ball in Cuba. A local lawman confronted them as they waited for a train outside the Miami station. "'Well,' he said, 'you niggers can't stand around here because you might rile up the white boys and we don't want trouble.' We had to call a Negro cab

Judy Johnson holds his plaque following his belated induction into the Hall of Fame. *Courtesy of Larry Lester/Negro Leagues Baseball Museum, Inc.*

because no one else would drive us, and we had to go to the Negro district and stay there four hours until it was time for our train."[26]

Even at the ballparks, aside from the usual racial slurs, there were other restrictions. In Rome, Georgia, Black Crackers manager Bill Yancey asked the clubhouse attendant where the team should dress. He was told that the locker rooms were closed and that "niggers" had to dress in nearby homes.[27] Some major league clubs also jealously guarded their locker room facilities from the black pros. The Pittsburgh Pirates, for example, would not allow black teams to use the locker rooms at Forbes Field. Black teams had to dress at a YMCA across town.[28]

Local white ball players, who were usually on the losing end of games with barnstorming blacks, often vented their pent-up hostility and frustration. While awaiting his turn at bat, William ("Sug") Cornelius, who was pitching a no-hitter one day in Dayton, Ohio, was called a "black sonofabitch" and hit by his white counterpart.[29]

Jeff Tesreau, an ex-New York Giant who opted for the richer semipro circuit by founding his own team, the Tesreau Bears, was a frequent opponent of New York's black teams. Once when confronting Louis Santop, a fellow Texan from his hometown of Tyler, Tesreau tried to bean the black catcher. When Santop yelled out for an explanation, Tesreau replied, "All niggers look alike to me."[30]

A potentially life-threatening situation involved black slugger George ("Mule") Suttles, playing in Claybrook, Arkansas, against the black hometown Tigers. A white man camped near the visitors' dugout with a gun. Telling the team what was and what was not acceptable, he told Suttles he had better put one over the fence or find a hole and crawl through it. Fortunately, the opposing pitcher, sensing the situation and hearing pleas from the dugout, served up Mule's favorite pitch and Suttles homered.[31]

Ironically, it was in the North that Judy Johnson got his greatest scare. Playing in Pennsylvania's coal region with the Hilldale team, the black pros were having an especially difficult time with the umpire, who also happened to be the local sheriff and made no secret of his disdain for the black visitors. Catcher Louis Santop visited the mound to call for a high, hard fastball. Santop made no attempt to catch the ball, which struck the lawman-umpire in the throat. It was to be that game's last pitch. The Negro leaguers made a run for their cars and were chased five or six miles down the road by the incensed local fans.[32]

Food was the biggest single problem for touring players. Being turned away from restaurants was a common occurrence. According to Quincy Trouppe, "Often we were told we could buy our food at the back kitchen door, and we had to take it off the property to eat it."[33] This was the norm. Jack Marshall of the Chicago American Giants recalled that even on trips to other league towns there was no place to stop and eat unless it was in a black community or in the black section of the city.[34]

Monte Irvin, who grew up in the North, found southern prejudice particularly difficult to understand. En route from Birmingham to Montgomery, the Newark Eagles bus stopped at a café. The café owner emerged shaking her head. "Why, you don't even know what we want," said Irvin. "Whatever it is, we don't have any," she replied. "Won't you even sell us some soft drinks?" he asked. "No!" she responded. Finally, one player remarked how hot it was and asked if they might get a drink from the well in the backyard. This she allowed, but as the bus pulled away, she could be seen breaking the drinking gourd the players had used. Irvin could not understand such unfounded hatred, but the black players to whom racism was a way of life didn't even think about it. To them it was a normal pattern of life in a segregated society.[35]

Undaunted, black athletes learned to bring their food with them. Beans and sardines combined in a bell jar with crackers seemed to be standard road fare. Players carefully guarded their food, as it was common practice to "borrow" from one another.

Jimmy Crutchfield recounted one story for author William Brashler. Pitcher Harry Kincannon stepped on the bus with a few pieces of fried chicken. After eating some, he stood up brandishing a borrowed pistol and told his teammates that anyone tasting his food would also taste lead. When Kincannon fell asleep, the gun slipped from his lap. One player emptied the gun, and they passed the chicken around. After eating, they collected the bones, tied them into a necklace, and placed it around Kincannon's neck. When he awoke, even the stunned pitcher joined in the laughter.[36]

Big League Competition

Many competitive black players regarded all the hardships of life on the road to be worth it when they got the chance to play against white major leaguers. Unquestionably, these games were the most psychologically and financially satisfying. Although most major leaguers made more money than their black contemporaries, they too felt the need to supplement their salaries with barnstorming circuits. Babe Ruth, Dizzy Dean, and Bob Feller were but three of many white stars who regularly formed postseason teams to display their talents to the radio-bound American public. Black teams represented quality competition with a national following. "They didn't allow Negroes in the majors," said former black umpire Frank Forbes, "but we were attractive to them in October. We would practically get more games with them in October than we could play."[37] Such competition assured not only fan appeal but good pay for the players—both black and white.

The games were a financial boon to the black players.

Paid on a game-by-game basis, generally they could be assured of earning about a month's salary for a single game. Ted Radcliffe estimated an average pay of $200 to $250 a game.[38] Games involving Satchel Paige versus Dizzy Dean or, later, Paige versus Bob Feller drew huge crowds, and the pay was superb. In 1941, Feller's all-stars played thirty-two games against black teams in twenty-six days before more than 400,000 fans. Long-time Saint Louis Cardinal player Stan Musial's share in the 1946 World Series was about $2,000, but Bob Feller's barnstormers earned about $6,000 each during that October.[39]

For their part, black players welcomed the opportunity to test themselves against the best in white baseball, and their 60 percent success rate was a ready source of pride. The greatest pitchers in the major leagues—Rube Wadell, Walter Johnson, Lefty Grove, Grover Cleveland Alexander, Dizzy Dean, Bob Feller, Bob Lemon—all lost games to black teams. Leon Day, a seventeen-year veteran of the Negro leagues, recalled: "We used to play harder against them than we did ourselves. We weren't allowed to play with them, but by beating them, we proved we could have."[40]

Recognition of their skills by their white counterparts provided a psychological lift for the black players as well. Dizzy Dean, a thirty-game winner in the National League, said to Satchel Paige after a loss, "You're a better pitcher 'n I ever hope to be, Satchel."[41] Earl Mack, the son of baseball owner Connie Mack, said to Cool Papa Bell, "If the door was open, you'd be the first guy I'd hire."[42] Memphis Red Sox catcher Larry Brown was asked if he would stay in Cuba and learn Spanish so that he could pass for a Latin American and be signed by the Detroit Tigers. Brown refused.[43] When Ted Williams was inducted into the Hall of Fame in 1966, he said, "I hope . . . Satchel Paige and Josh Gibson will be voted into the Hall of Fame as symbols of the great Negro players who are not here only because they weren't given the chance."

Finally, worthy of note, given the prevailing argument that whites and blacks could not play together, was the relatively little racial friction between pro black and white opponents. This prompted Lenny Pearson of the Newark Eagles to observe, "You can't blame the white ballplayers, because I think if it was left entirely to them—I won't say all the ballplayers, but the majority—they wouldn't have had any qualms about playing with colored players."[44]

Games between professional black and white players were profitable for players of both colors; however, money could not eliminate prejudice. After losing to a black team in a barnstorming game in California, Detroit Tiger pitcher Bobo Newsome commented, "I'm not going back . . . 'til I beat these niggers." Cool Papa Bell, standing nearby, responded, "We're gonna keep you here 'bout two more years."[45]

And some black players were not above showing up a white. When Chicago Cub player Frank Demaree made a slur about a Satchel Paige team during a game, Paige responded with his arm, not his mouth. He deliberately walked three players to get to Demaree. When Demaree stepped to the plate, Paige called in his outfielders and told his infielders to sit down. He then proceeded to strike out Demaree on three pitches.

On July 21, 1942, Satchel Paige again walked men to get at a hitter, but for a very different reason. Years before, when Satchel and Josh Gibson had been young teammates with the Pittsburgh Crawfords, Satchel, never a modest man, had said to Gibson, "Some day we're gonna meet up. You're the greatest hitter . . . and I'm the greatest pitcher, and we're gonna see who's best." So on this July day, which Paige chose for a showdown, he and the Monarchs were leading Gibson and the Grays 4–0 going into the seventh inning. With two down, leadoff man Jerry Benjamin tripled. Paige then deliberately walked two batters to get to Gibson amid cheers from the crowd, who realized what he was doing. He reminded Gibson of their conversation years before and then threw two fastballs that Gibson took for called strikes. Before throwing the next pitch, Satchel called out, "Now Josh, that's two strikes. Now I'm not going to try to trick you. I'm not gonna throw any smoke around your yoke. I'm gonna throw a pea on your knee, only it's gonna be faster than the last one." He then threw a knee-high fastball on the outside corner that Gibson took for strike three.[46]

SIX

The Integration of Baseball

B y 1945, many black Americans were ready to de-
mand the equality and total integration that Booker
T. Washington had predicted would come. Their
political strength had grown during President Franklin Roosevelt's New Deal years. Both Roosevelt and his wife,
Eleanor, were sympathetic to black causes. The new admin-
istration sought the advice of many blacks and appointed a
number of them to significant positions. The growing political strength of blacks was evident when Arthur Miller was
elected to the House of Representatives in 1934. Miller was
the first African-American Democrat to sit in the United
States Congress. His election, which was an embarrassment
to the coalition of southern Democrats in Congress, was
regarded as a victory by blacks across the land.

Sensing the growing political strength of blacks, A.
Philip Randolph, president of the Brotherhood of Sleeping
Car Porters, began to organize a march on Washington,
D.C., in 1941 to protest the failure of many defense industries to hire blacks. Randolph's threat was a major factor in
motivating President Roosevelt to sign an executive order
forbidding discrimination in hiring in defense industries and
government.

During World War II, although most fighting units were

segregated, blacks were accepted for the first time into officer candidate schools, the air force, and the marines. In January 1945, black and white troops were organized into integrated units to fight in Germany. In 1949, following an investigation ordered by President Harry Truman, the armed services were integrated.

The Erosion of Jim Crowism in Baseball

The increasing power of the black community was illustrated by a baseball-related incident. During a pregame radio interview in July 1938, Jake Powell, a New York Yankees outfielder, responded to a question about his off-season occupation by saying that he stayed in shape "cracking niggers over the head" for the Chicago police department. The show was immediately cut off. In response to protests by Chicago's black population, Powell was suspended for ten days. After his return, he was booed at games throughout August and became the target of bottle-throwing fans.

Sportswriters used the affair to point out that Powell's remarks, while indefensible, in a sense reflected the view of major league owners, who refused to sign black players. Although most white fans were generally unaware of the Negro leagues, sportswriters, particularly black sportswriters, knew that some players in the Negro leagues were better than many whites wearing major league uniforms.

During World War II, when unemployment, even among minorities, was minimal, black workers packed the stands at Negro league ball parks to watch many of the star black players who were too old to be drafted into the army. Meanwhile, attendance at major league parks declined as star players went off to war. Clark Griffith, owner of the lowly Washington Senators, who were especially hard hit by poor attendance, met with Josh Gibson and Buck Leonard of the Homestead Grays. The Grays were using Griffith Stadium as their home field and outdrawing the Senators. Griffith asked Gibson and Leonard if they would like to play for the Senators. He made no commitment, but rumors began to fly that the Senators were about to hire black players. These rumors led reporters for the *Pittsburgh Courier* to discuss the possibility of hiring black players with Bill Benswanger, owner of the Pirates. Benswanger admitted that adding black players might help the quality of major league play, but neither he nor Griffith ever dared to make the move.

Leo Durocher, an outspoken major league manager, made it known that he'd be happy to have black players if owners would sign them. Feeling somewhat threatened by Durocher's comments, Commissioner Kenesaw Mountain Landis stated that there was no rule barring any race from the major leagues and that he was not opposed to the integration of professional baseball.

Landis's words, however, were quite different from his actions. In 1943, Bill Veeck made arrangements to buy the Philadelphia Phillies from owner Jerry Nugent. Veeck planned to improve the Phillies' dismal record by hiring a number of black players. As a courtesy, he went to see Judge Landis in New York to tell him of his plans. Following what he thought was a cordial meeting, Veeck learned the next morning that the National League had taken over the Phillies until a suitable owner could be found. Landis had quickly found a subtle way to avoid integration in the major leagues by circumventing Veeck's purchase and buying time for the league to find another investor.

Following the death of Landis in 1944, Kentucky Senator Albert ("Happy") Chandler became the commissioner of baseball. Chandler had stated several times that if blacks

The one–two punch of the Homestead Grays—Buck Leonard *(left)* and Josh Gibson *(right). Courtesy of Larry Lester/Negro Leagues Baseball Museum, Inc.*

could fight in the country's wars, they were certainly entitled to play on major league teams. With Chandler in charge, the probability of seeing integrated major league teams improved dramatically. In fact, three black players—Jackie Robinson, Sam Jethroe, and Marvin Williams—were invited to Boston to try out for the Red Sox.

It's doubtful, however, that the Red Sox had any intention of signing a black player. The team was probably trying to appease a group made up of Boston liberals and traditional opponents of Sunday baseball. The group was threatening to fight for the banning of Sunday baseball in Boston unless blacks were given the opportunity to play major league ball.

Jackie Robinson and Branch Rickey

In 1945, Branch Rickey, general manager of the Brooklyn Dodgers (now the Los Angeles Dodgers), proposed establishing the United States Baseball League. It would be made up of black teams, including the Brooklyn Brown Dodgers, that would play at Ebbetts Field while the major league team was on the road. The other New York teams, the Giants and the Yankees, already rented their stadiums to black teams. In fact, rental income for Yankee Stadium, largely from black teams, was about $100,000 per year, more than some teams' entire profits from their own games. But Rickey's promotion was more than a money-making scheme. He was preparing to bring black players into the National League. Promoting the Brown Dodgers gave him the opportunity to scout blacks without suspicion.

Several factors led Rickey to begin his search for a black who could play for the Dodgers. He knew that attendance at Negro National and American League games was often larger than at many major league parks. A black player would be a big drawing card for New York's minority population. And, like other New York teams, he was being pressured to sign black players by the State Fair Employment Practices Committee, sportswriters, and New York mayor Fiorello La Guardia's Anti-Discrimination Committee. Rickey was also a man with a conscience; he realized that barring players from baseball because of their color was unfair, if not immoral. But he wanted to be certain that the first player to break the color barrier would be successful. Therefore, he sought someone who would be a star both on and off the field, someone whose play would be outstanding and whose behavior would be exemplary. With Rickey's qualifications in mind, Brooklyn scouts began searching the black leagues. Their choice was Jackie Robinson, a young player with the Kansas City Monarchs.

Robinson had been an outstanding athlete in baseball, football, basketball, and track in high school, at Pasadena Junior College, and at UCLA. During his senior year at UCLA he starred in football and was widely regarded as the best all-around athlete on the West Coast. After three years of limited service in the army (he had bone chips in his ankle), he was discharged as a second lieutenant. Shortly thereafter, in April 1945, he began playing for the Kansas City Monarchs at a salary of $400 a month.

In forty-one games with the Monarchs, Robinson batted .345; had ten doubles, four triples, and five home runs; and was selected to play shortstop for the West in the annual East-West All-star Game. Rickey's scouts reported that he was a good batter and runner, possessed outstanding baseball sense and intelligence, but had difficulty making plays to his right as a shortstop. They suggested that he play first or second base. Furthermore, Robinson, like Rickey, was a teetotaler.

Pleased with the scouting reports, Rickey himself went to California to talk with people who knew Robinson. Their only criticism was that Jackie would stand up for his rights and would not tolerate Jim Crowism. In late August 1945, Brooklyn scout Clyde Sukeforth asked Robinson to come to Brooklyn to meet Rickey. Robinson thought Rickey wanted to hire him to play for the Brown Dodgers, but when Montreal, a Brooklyn Dodger farm team, was mentioned, Robinson knew he had been chosen to break the color barrier.

Rickey went on at great length about the prejudice and pressure that Robinson would have to endure both on and off the field. When Robinson asked if Rickey were looking for someone who was afraid to fight back, Rickey replied that he was looking for someone with guts enough *not* to fight back.

Robinson agreed to play with Montreal in 1946 for $600 a month and a $3,500 bonus. A formal contract was signed in Montreal on October 23, 1945, and Robinson opened the 1946 season with Montreal's International League team at Jersey City's Roosevelt Stadium on April 18. It had been fifty-seven years since a black had played in the International League and forty-eight in any recognized minor league. After grounding to short in his first at bat, Robinson collected four hits, including a home run, stole two bases, and was waved home twice from third base when pitchers, disconcerted by his base running, committed balks.

Watching from the Montreal dugout was John Wright. He would become the second black to play in organized baseball in the twentieth century. Wright had been signed by the Dodgers organization in February.

In the spring of 1946, Robinson and Wright endured racism in Florida and actually had to be removed from one game because local laws forbid competition between blacks and whites. During the season, racial abuse from fans and opposing players was common, but Robinson enjoyed amazing success. He led the league with a .349 batting average, was second in stolen bases with forty, and led the league in runs scored with 113.

John Wright did not fare as well. After two relief appearances, he was sent to Three Rivers, a class C team. He was released the next winter and rejoined the Homestead Grays.

In 1947, the Dodgers held their spring training in Cuba to avoid racism and the extensive publicity sure to accompany the purchase of Jackie Robinson's contract from their Montreal farm club. After it was announced that Robinson would play in Brooklyn, six Dodgers veterans threatened not to play with Robinson. Branch Rickey met with each player and told him in no uncertain terms that he *would* play with Robinson or be fired.

The black community was thrilled to learn that Robinson had broken the color barrier. But professional black players, while sharing in the excitement, questioned the choice of Robinson, a rookie. There were, they felt, plenty of experienced, proven players like Josh Gibson and Satchel Paige who were more deserving of the opportunity than Robinson. They believed Robinson had been chosen because he had played football with whites. Although there were players in the Negro leagues who were better than Robinson, there was more to Rickey's choice than ability. Character and mental toughness were prime factors as well.

At Ebbets Field on opening day, April 15, 1947, Jackie Robinson was the Brooklyn Dodgers first baseman. He went hitless but scored the fifth run in a 5–3 win over the Boston

Braves (now the Atlanta Braves). Early in the season, the Philadelphia Phillies and St. Louis Cardinals threatened to strike rather than play on the same field with Robinson. Ford Frick, president of the National League, wrote to the Cardinals informing them that anyone who refused to play against Robinson would be suspended. Forced to play against Robinson, opposing bench jockeys were quick to test his temper. They called him "snowflake" and "nigger" and shouted for him to go back to the cotton fields where he belonged. As Rickey had requested, Robinson endured it all, showing that he had sufficient courage *not* to fight back.

Robinson led the Dodgers to the 1947 pennant, finishing the season with a .297 batting average, twelve home runs, twenty-nine stolen bases, and 125 runs scored. Even Dixie Walker, a southerner and one of the players who had threatened to strike during spring training, said that Robinson had done as much as anyone to bring Brooklyn to the top of the National League.

Rickey had chosen the right man to break the color ban. Being the first to break the color barrier had a price that few would have paid. In addition to the usual pressures faced by any rookie, Robinson had to endure sullen teammates, racial slurs, hate mail, threats of assaults on him and his family, including the threatened kidnapping of his infant son. Robinson had the mental toughness and courage to endure as well as the intelligence to view his situation from a broad perspective. Even those black players who felt they should have been chosen ahead of Robinson respected and admired his heart, spirit, determination, and all that he had accomplished. They realized he had made it easier for those who would follow.

Those Who Followed

In April 1946, the Brooklyn Dodgers announced that two more blacks, Roy Campanella and Don Newcombe, had signed with the Dodgers organization. This put to rest the cynical remarks of many white players who maintained that Wright had been signed in February just to keep Robinson company. It was clear now that Rickey's move was more than a publicity stunt. He fully intended to integrate the Brooklyn Dodgers.

Campanella was twenty-four years old with nine years of experience catching in the Negro leagues. Newcombe was a big, hard-throwing nineteen-year-old pitcher who at six feet, four inches stood a full seven inches taller than the man who was to be his catcher and roommate. After receiving their indoctrination lecture from Branch Rickey, both were assigned to the Nashua, New Hampshire, Dodgers. Their manager was Walter Alston, who later followed his black stars to the major leagues.

Campanella, who batted .290 that season and led Nashua with thirteen homers and ninety-six RBIs, was chosen all-league catcher. Newcombe sported a 14–4 pitching record with a 2.21 ERA and was the team's most effective pinch hitter. During the season, Alston asked Campanella, who was the most experienced player on the squad, to assume managerial duties if he (Alston) were ever thrown out of a game. Several weeks later, after Alston was ejected from the game by an umpire, Campanella took over. Trailing Lawrence by one run, Campy sent his roommate to the plate as a pinch hitter. Newcombe made Campanella's managerial record 1–0 by stroking a home run.

In a town where black men were few, Nashua's citizens

treated both men well. The local barber even tried to cut their hair—not very well, to be sure, because his clientele had always been 100 percent white. Opposing players would sometimes hurl racial epithets at Newcombe and Campanella, who were able to ignore the name calling and respond with their bats and arms, not their mouths and fists. Unlike Robinson, who had to dodge beanballs throughout the season with Montreal, Campanella and Newcombe were seldom brushed back. With Newcombe's speed and tendency to be a bit wild, no opposing pitcher or manager dared throw at either player.

In 1947, Campanella was moved up to Montreal, while Newcombe remained in Nashua for another year of experience under Alston's tutelage. By 1949, Robinson, Campanella, and Newcombe were all-star players for the Brooklyn Dodgers and there were thirty-six black players in the major and minor leagues.

After John Wright arrived at Three Rivers in 1946, he was joined by Roy Partlow, another black player who had been signed by the Dodgers organization. Parlow had an outstanding 10–1 season at Three Rivers, batted .404, and pitched magnificently in the championship series, where his arm and bat were instrumental in beating Pittsfield four games to one in a seven-game playoff series. The following year Partlow joined Campanella at Montreal.

Bill Veeck, who had failed in his bid to buy the Phillies, was the owner of the Cleveland Indians in 1947 when they purchased Larry Doby from the Newark Eagles. Doby, who was leading the Negro National League with a .415 average and fourteen home runs, became, on July 5, 1947, the first black to break the American League color barrier. For the most part, his teammates were cordial but not friendly. However, Lou Boudreau, Cleveland's playing manager, treated him well and warmed up with him before games. Joe Gordon, the veteran second baseman, encouraged Doby on the field and offered extensive help with his fielding. In return for his support, Doby would always pick up Gordon's glove and throw it to him when they went out onto the field after Cleveland's turn at bat. (In those days, players left their gloves on the field when they came in to bat.)

On the road, Doby, the only black on the Cleveland team, roomed alone. During road trips to Chicago and St. Louis, he had to live in black boarding houses because the hotels in these cities refused him a room. But in Washington, D.C., the Hotel Statler, which had always refused blacks, accepted him as their first black guest. His loneliness on the road was relieved by frequent telephone conversations with Jackie Robinson. The two provided helpful support to one another during their stressful first seasons in the majors.

On July 16, 1947, the St. Louis Browns, twenty-six games out of first place and sometimes attracting fewer than five hundred fans, became the third major league team to sign black players. They purchased Hank Thompson and Willard Brown for a trial period from the Kansas City Monarchs and obtained a thirty-day option on Piper Davis of the Birmingham Black Barons. Both Brown and Thompson were unhappy in St. Louis. Despite the racist attitude of many of the Browns players, management had taken no time to prepare the team for the two blacks who suddenly appeared in the St. Louis locker room. When Brown and Thompson failed to lift the Browns out of the cellar or attract more hometown fans, they were released and the Browns dropped the option on Davis. Two years later, Thompson was signed by the New York Giants and remained in the majors for eight years.

Jackie Robinson once said that in breaking baseball's

color barrier, Branch Rickey did more for blacks than any white man since Abraham Lincoln. And the black athletes who benefited from Rickey's actions served as the agents of integration. Integrated professional teams traveling through the South challenged Jim Crowism. "Integration in baseball," claimed Rickey, "started public integration on trains, in Pullmans, in dining cars, in restaurants in the South, long before the issue of public accommodation became daily news."[1]

The End of the Negro Leagues

In July 1949, when Satchel Paige signed with the Cleveland Indians and helped them to win the pennant, few black teams were making money. Without players of Paige's stature and drawing power, attendance at black games dwindled. The fans who had filled the parks of the Negro leagues now wanted to see the black players who had made it to the majors. Only by selling players to major league franchises could black teams stay afloat. Top players like Dan Bankhead, who went to the Dodgers organization in 1947, and Willie Mays, who was signed by the New York Giants in 1950, might bring $15,000. But it was clear that the Negro leagues were simply developing talent for the majors. When major league clubs began signing players to their farm teams right out of high school, the Negro leagues had no role left. By 1960, the Negro American League consisted of only four teams—the Kansas City Monarchs, the Detroit-New Orleans Stars, the Birmingham Black Barons, and the Raleigh Tigers. It was the league's final year.

Jackie Robinson and the other black players who followed him had made Rube Foster's dream a reality. Competent black players now had the chance to not only

Satchel Paige, black baseball's first Hall of Famer. *Courtesy of Larry Lester/ Negro Leagues Baseball Museum, Inc.*

compete but excel in the major leagues, and they made the most of the opportunity. Hank Aaron, a former member of the Indianapolis Clowns, holds the record for most home runs in a career—755. Roy Campanella, who had played with the Baltimore Elite Giants, won the National League's most valuable player (MVP) award three times. Former Newark Eagle Don Newcombe was a Cy Young award winner and the National League's MVP in 1956. Ernie Banks, who started his career with the Kansas City Monarchs, won back-

Cool Papa Bell, shown here with a big bat, was better known for speed than power. *Courtesy of Larry Lester/Negro Leagues Baseball Museum, Inc.*

to-back MVP awards in 1958 and 1959—the only player on a losing team (the Chicago Cubs) ever to do so.

The testimony of former white major leaguers and black players who entered the majors after 1947 made it clear that the black major league award winners were but a small sample of the talent to be found in the Negro leagues. Other highly skilled black players, still unrecognized by the

Mainstays of the Pittsburgh Crawfords' lineup in the thirties include three now in baseball's Hall of Fame. *From left to right:* Oscar Charleston, Josh Gibson, Ted Page, and Judy Johnson. *Courtesy of National Baseball Library, Cooperstown, N.Y.*

white baseball establishment, who played in the Negro leagues during the first half of the twentieth century deserved to be in the Baseball Hall of Fame. In 1971, when Satchel Paige was admitted to the Hall of Fame, the cry of fairness in recognizing baseball's greatest players was heard at last. Since that time, through the action of the Special Committee on Negro Leagues and the New Veterans Committee, nine other players from the Negro leagues are now in the Baseball Hall of Fame—Josh Gibson, Buck Leonard, Judy Johnson, James "Cool Papa" Bell, Oscar Charleston,

Martin Dihigo, John Henry Lloyd, Rube Foster, and Ray Dandridge.

The admission of these players is a step in the right direction, but there are other qualified black players whose talents should be recognized. The claim that there are no statistics on other players is being addressed by the Society for American Baseball Research.[2] Their efforts to date show that Bill Foster, Rube's brother, had more Negro league victories than Satchel Paige. And both Foster and Andy Cooper, a quiet, relatively unknown pitcher, had better over-all records than the flamboyant Paige. Their research has also shown that Norman ("Turkey") Stearns and George ("Mule") Suttles hit more league homers than either Oscar Charleston or Josh Gibson. These players, along with Willie Wells, Dave Malarcher, "Smokey" Joe Williams, Dick Redding, Jimmy Crutchfield, and others deserve places in the Hall of Fame as well.

 **NOTES**

Introduction

1. Donn Rogosin, "Queen of the Negro Leagues," *Sportscape,* Summer 1981 (Cooperstown, N.Y.: Baseball Hall of Fame Library), p. 17.
2. Effa Manley and Leon Herbert Hardwick, *Negro Baseball Before Integration* (Chicago: Adams Press), 1976, p. 5.

Chapter 2

1. Robert Peterson, *Only the Ball Was White* (New York: McGraw-Hill, 1970), p. 105.
2. Ibid.
3. John Holway, *Rube Foster: The Father of Black Baseball* (Washington, D.C.: Pretty Pages, 1982), p. 4.
4. Ibid., p. 6.
5. John Holway, "Rube Foster, Father of the Black Game" (*Sporting News,* August 8, 1981), p. 19.
6. Peterson, *Only the Ball Was White,* p. 107.
7. Holway, *Rube Foster: The Father of Black Baseball,* p. 9.
8. "Historically Speaking: The Negro Baseball Leagues" (*Black Sports,* May/June 1971), p. 74.
9. Jeffrey Eliot, "Quincy Trouppe: Portrait of a Super-Star" (*Negro History Bulletin,* March/April 1978), p. 805.
10. Holway, "Rube Foster, Father of the Black Game," p. 19.
11. Earl Foster, *Andrew "Rube" Foster Scrapbook* (Cooperstown, N.Y.: Baseball Hall of Fame Library), p. 8.
12. Ibid.
13. Ibid., p. 17.

14. "Royal Giants Are Ousted and Reinstated in Colored League" (*The New York Age,* May 31, 1924), p. 7.
15. Holway, "Rube Foster, Father of the Black Game," p. 20.
16. Peterson, *Only the Ball Was White,* pp. 109–10.
17. Earl Foster, interview with Robert Peterson (Cooperstown, N.Y.: Baseball Hall of Fame Library).
18. Holway, *Rube Foster: The Father of Black Baseball,* p. 15.
19. Ibid., p. 13.
20. Ibid., p. 12.
21. John Holway, "Bill Holland" (*New York Folklore Quarterly,* 1971), p. 307.
22. Holway, *Rube Foster: The Father of Black Baseball,* p. 18.
23. Ibid., p. 17.
24. Ibid., p. 23.
25. Donn Rogosin, *Invisible Men: Life in Baseball's Negro Leagues* (New York: Atheneum, 1983), p. 34.
26. Holway, *Rube Foster: The Father of Black Baseball,* p. 24.

Chapter 3

1. John Holway, *Voices from the Great Black Baseball Leagues* (New York: Dodd Mead, 1975), p. 194.
2. Rogosin, *Invisible Men: Life in Baseball's Negro Leagues,* pp. 17, 104.
3. Rogosin, "Queen of the Negro Leagues," p. 18.
4. "Josh the Basher" (*Time,* July 19, 1943), p. 75.
5. Rogosin, *Invisible Men: Life in Baseball's Negro Leagues,* p. 104.
6. Rogosin, "Queen of the Negro Leagues," p. 18.
7. "Jake" Paul Stephens, interview with John Holway (Cooperstown, N.Y.: Baseball Hall of Fame Library), p. 6.

8. Donn Rogosin, "Black Baseball, Life in the Negro Leagues" (Ph.D. dissertation, University of Texas, 1981), p. 50.
9. John Coates II and Merl Kleinknecht, "Historically Speaking: Martin Dihigo," (*Black Sports,* November, 1973), p. 13.

Chapter 4

1. Jeffrey Eliot, "It's Time to Finish Taking Racism Out of Pro Baseball" (*Sepia,* December 1977), p. 29.
2. John Holway, "Negro League Reunion: Paige and Pals" (*Washington Sunday Star,* June 28, 1981), from clipping in Baseball Hall of Fame Library files on Negro leagues.
3. John Holway, "Louis Santop, The Big Bertha" (*Baseball Research Journal,* 1979), p. 94.
4. John Holway, *Voices from the Great Black Baseball Leagues* (New York: Dodd Mead, 1975), p. 302.
5. Clipping from Joe Williams file at Baseball Hall of Fame Library, Cooperstown, N.Y.
6. Holway, *Voices From the Great Black Baseball Leagues,* p. 162.
7. Roy Campanella, *It's Good To Be Alive* (Boston: Little, Brown, 1959), p. 84.
8. Buck Leonard, interview with Robert Peterson (Cooperstown, N.Y.: Baseball Hall of Fame Library), p. 3.
9. John Holway, "Historically Speaking: Bill Foster" (*Black Sports,* March, 1974), p. 58.
10. John Holway, *Smokey Joe and The Cannonball* (Washington, D.C.: Capital Press, 1983), p. 26.
11. Robert Peterson, "Josh Gibson Was the Equal of Babe Ruth, But," *New York Times Magazine,* April 11, 1971, p. 30.

12. Dwayne Cheeks, "The Cleveland Buckeyes Remembered: Played Second Fiddle to Tribe Until Demise" (*Cleveland Plain Dealer,* January 18, 1982), p. 80.
13. Al Harvin, "Historically Speaking: Judy Johnson" (*Black Sports,* April, 1975), p. 52.
14. Holway, *Smokey Joe and The Cannonball,* p. 6.
15. John Holway, "Vic Harris Managed Homestead Grays" (*Dawn Magazine,* March 8, 1975), p. 12.
16. Dr. Charles Korr, Irene Cortinovis, Dr. Stephen House, and Len Licata, "Oral History Interview with Bill Drake" (Cooperstown, N.Y.: Baseball Hall of Fame Library).
17. Holway, *Voices From the Great Black Baseball Leagues,* p. 114.
18. Campanella, *It's Good To Be Alive,* p. 70.
19. Mark Kram, "It Seemed Like It Happened in Another Century" (*Baltimore News American,* August 9, 1981), p. 2E.
20. Rogosin, *Invisible Men: Life in Baseball's Negro Leagues,* p. 72.
21. Holway, *Smokey Joe and The Cannonball,* p. 7.
22. John Holway, "Dobie Moore" (*Baseball Research Journal,* 1981), p. 170.
23. "Jake" Paul Stephens, interview with John Holway, p. 11.
24. John Holway, "Historically Speaking: Jelly Gardner" (*Black Sports,* September, 1974), p. 60.
25. "Jake" Paul Stephens, interview with John Holway, p. 23.
26. John Holway, "Historically Speaking: Frank Duncan: The Complete Catcher" (*Black Sports,* December, 1973), p. 22.
27. Holway, *Voices from the Great Black Baseball Leagues,* p. 94.

28. Ibid.
29. Ibid., p. 346.
30. John M. Coates, "Historically Speaking: James Bell" (*Black Sports,* October, 1973), p. 11.
31. Foster, *Andrew "Rube" Foster Scrapbook,* p. 18.
32. "Eastern Colored League May Be Abandoned Next Season, Says Nat Strong" (*New York Age,* August 7, 1926), p. 6.
33. Holway, *Voices from the Great Black Baseball Leagues,* p. 34.
34. Horace G. Hall, interview with Robert Peterson (Coopers-town, N.Y.: Baseball Hall of Fame Library), p. 1.
35. Rogosin, *Invisible Men: Life in Baseball's Negro Leagues,* pp. 26–27.
36. David Malarcher, Letter to Robert Peterson, November 20, 1968 (Cooperstown, N.Y.: Baseball Hall of Fame Library).
37. Kram, "It Seemed Like It Happened in Another Century," p. 3E.
38. Brashler, *Josh Gibson: A Life in the Negro Leagues,* pp. 73–74.
39. Eliot, "It's Time to Finish Taking Racism Out of Pro Baseball," p. 31.
40. John Holway, "Not All Stars Were White" (*Sporting News,* July 4, 1983, Special All-star Section), p. 4.
41. Holway, *Voices from the Great Black Baseball Leagues,* p. 349.
42. Ibid., p. 84.
43. Art Carter, "From the Bench" (*Afro Sports,* January 11, 1941: Cooperstown, N.Y.: Baseball Hall of Fame Library, Negro League File).
44. Holway, "Historically Speaking: Frank Duncan: The Complete Catcher," p. 54.

45. Leroy (Satchel) Paige, *Maybe I'll Pitch Forever* (Garden City, N.Y.: Doubleday, 1962), p. 78.

Chapter 5

1. Bob Broeg, "Broeg on Baseball: Lloyd and Dihigo Had Talent to Burn" (*The Sporting News*, March 19, 1977; Cooperstown, N.Y.: Baseball Hall of Fame Library, Martin Dihigo File).
2. Paul W. Fisher, "Talk of the Times" (Cooperstown, N.Y.: Baseball Hall of Fame Library, John Coates III File).
3. William Brashler, *Josh Gibson: A Life in the Negro Leagues* (New York: Harper and Row, 1978), p. 65.
4. Harlan Joye, Cliff Kuhn, and Bernard West, *The Atlanta Black Crackers* (cassettes) (Atlanta: WRGF Living Atlanta Project, 1978).
5. Robert Peter, File on Dick Redding (Cooperstown, N.Y.: Baseball Hall of Fame Library).
6. "Felton Snow Recalls 'The Black Babe Ruth,'" (Cooperstown, N.Y.: Baseball Hall of Fame Library, Josh Gibson File).
7. Jim Kaplan, "Bittersweet Barnstorming" (*Sports Illustrated*, February 16, 1981), p. 45.
8. Jack Lang, "Johnson, 'Black Traynor,' Elected to Shrine" (*The Sporting News*, March 1, 1975; Cooperstown, N.Y.: Baseball Hall of Fame Library, Judy Johnson File).
9. Cheeks, "The Cleveland Buckeyes Remembered: Played Second Fiddle to Tribe Until Demise," p. 70.
10. "The Man: Monte Irvin," *Black Sports*, July, 1971, p. 21.
11. Kram, "It Seemed Like It Happened in Another Century," p. 3E.
12. Peterson, "Josh Gibson Was the Equal of Babe Ruth, But," p. 30.

13. F. Kelly, "Judy Johnson: From Snow Hill to the Hall of Fame" (Cooperstown, N.Y.: Baseball Hall of Fame Library, Judy Johnson File).
14. Cheeks, "The Cleveland Buckeyes Remembered: Played Second Fiddle to Tribe Until Demise," p. 80.
15. Judy Johnson, interview with Robert Peterson (Cooperstown, N.Y.: Baseball Hall of Fame Library).
16. Theodore Rosengarten, "Reading the Hops: Recollections of Lorenzo 'Piper' Davis and the Negro Baseball League" (*Southern Exposure,* Summer/Fall, 1977), p. 71.
17. Peterson, "Josh Gibson Was the Equal of Babe Ruth, But," p. 30.
18. Joye, Kuhn, and West, *The Atlanta Black Crackers* (cassettes).
19. Ibid.
20. Ibid.
21. Stephen Banker (Interviewer), *Black Diamonds: An Oral History of Negro Baseball* (cassettes), (Princeton, N.J.: Video Education Corporation, 1978).
22. Barry Jacobs, "Buck Leonard" (*Baseball America,* June 1, 1983), p. 5.
23. Banker, *Black Diamonds: An Oral History of Negro Baseball.*
24. Joye, Kuhn, and West, *The Atlanta Black Crackers.*
25. F. Kelly, "Judy Johnson: From Snow Hill to the Hall of Fame," Judy Johnson File.
26. Frederick Kelly, "Of Greatness Confined to a Harsher Time" (*Philadelphia Inquirer,* September 11, 1978), p. 4C.
27. Bill Yancey, interview with Robert Peterson (Cooperstown, N.Y.: Baseball Hall of Fame Library), p. 7.

28. Brashler, *Josh Gibson: A Life in the Negro Leagues,* p. 59.
29. John Holway, "Before You Could Say Jackie Robinson" (*Look,* July 13, 1971), p. 48.
30. Holway, "Louis Santop, The Big Bertha," p. 96.
31. Banker, *Black Diamonds: An Oral History of Negro Baseball.*
32. Ibid.
33. Eliot, "It's Time to Finish Taking Racism Out of Pro Baseball," p. 30.
34. Banker, *Black Diamonds: An Oral History of Negro Baseball.*
35. Rogosin, *Invisible Men: Life in Baseball's Negro Leagues,* p. 129.
36. Brashler, *Josh Gibson: A Life in the Negro Leagues,* p. 67.
37. Holway, *Smokey Joe and The Cannonball,* p. 7.
38. Banker, *Black Diamonds: An Oral History of Negro Baseball.*
39. Holway, *Voices from the Great Black Baseball Leagues,* p. 293.
40. Kram, "It Seemed Like It Happened in Another Century," p. 3E.
41. Leroy (Satchel) Paige, "Maybe I'll Pitch Forever," as told to Donald Lipman (*Saturday Evening Post,* March 11, 1961), p. 107.
42. Holway, *Voices from the Great Black Baseball Leagues,* p. 125.
43. Robert Peterson Files (Cooperstown, N.Y.: Baseball Hall of Fame).
44. Holway, "Before You Could Say Jackie Robinson," p. 49.
45. Rogosin, *Invisible Men: Life in Baseball's Negro Leagues,* p. 129.
46. *Sporting News,* July 18, 1981.

Chapter 6

1. Jules Tygiel, "Those Who Came After" (*Sports Illustrated,* June 27, 1983), p. 57.
2. John B. Holway, "Stats Shine on Stars of Negro Leagues" (*USA Today Baseball Weekly,* June 14–20, 1991), p. 48.

BIBLIOGRAPHY

Brashler, William. *Josh Gibson: A Life in the Negro Leagues.* New York: Harper and Row, 1978.

Bruce, Janet. *The Kansas City Monarchs: Champions of Black Baseball.* Kansas: University Press of Kansas, 1985.

Campanella, Roy. *It's Good To Be Alive.* Boston: Little, Brown, 1959.

Dixon, Phil, and Hannigan, Pat. *Negro Baseball Leagues: A Photographic History.* Mattituck, N.Y.: Amereon Ltd., 1990.

Holway, John B. *Blackball Stars: Negro League Pioneers.* Wesport, Conn.: Meckler Corp., 1988.

————. *Black Diamonds.* Westport, Conn.: Meckler Corp., 1989.

————. *Rube Foster: The Father of Black Baseball.* Washington, D.C.: Pretty Pages, 1982.

————. *Voices From the Great Black Baseball Leagues.* New York: Dodd Mead, 1975.

Johnson, Spencer. *The Value of Courage: The Story of Jackie Robinson.* Wilton, Conn.: Value Publishing, 1984.

Moore, Joseph T. *Pride Against Prejudice: The Biography of Larry Doby.* Charlotte, Vt.: Camden House, 1984.

Nash, Bruce, and Zullo, Allan. *The Baseball Hall of Shame: Young Fan's Edition.* New York: Pocket Books, 1990.

Peterson, Robert. *Only the Ball Was White.* New York: McGraw-Hill, 1970.

Riley, James A. *The All-Time All-Stars of Black Baseball.* Cocoa, Fla.: TK Pubs., 1983.

Rogosin, Donn. *Invisible Men: Life in Baseball's Negro Leagues.* New York: Atheneum, 1983.

Tygiel, Jules. *Baseball's Great Experiment: Jackie Robinson and His Legacy.* New York: Oxford Univ. Press, 1983.

Walker, Paul R. *Pride of Puerto Rico: The Life of Roberto Clemente.* San Diego: Harcourt Brace, 1988.

INDEX

Note: Page numbers in italics refer to photographs.